WHAT ARE THEY SAYING ABOUT
PAUL AND THE LAW?

What Are They Saying About Paul and the Law?

Veronica Koperski

PAULIST PRESS
NewYork/Mahwah, N.J.

Acknowledgment
"We Thank You Gracious God" by Robert A. Rimbo, copyright The Liturgical Conference. All rights reserved. Used with permission.

Cover design by James Brisson

Library of Congress Cataloging-in-Publication Data

Koperski, Veronica.
    What are they saying about Paul and the law? / Veronica Koperski.
        p.   cm. — (WATSA series)
    Includes bibliographical references and indexes.
    ISBN 0-8091-3965-0
    1. Paul, the Apostle, Saint—Views on Jewish law. 2. Jewish law. 3. Bible. N.T. Epistles of Paul—Criticism, interpretation, etc.—History—20th century. I. Title. II. Series.

BS2655.L35 K67 2000
225.9′2—dc21

                                                                00-062320

Published by Paulist Press
997 Macarthur Boulevard
Mahwah, New Jersey 07430

www.paulistpress.com

Printed and bound in the
United States of America

Contents

To Virginia Sloyan,
Laura Armesto,
and
Mark Wedig, O.P.

Abbreviations

AB   Anchor Bible

ALGHJ   Arbeiten zur Literatur und Geschichte des Hel-
            lenistischen Judentums

AnBib   Analecta Biblica

BA:OSA   Bibliothèque Augustinienne: Oeuvres de Saint
            Augustin

BETL   Bibliotheca Ephemeridum Theologicarum
            Lovaniensium

Bib   *Biblica*

BBR   *Bulletin for Biblical Research*

BJRL   *Bulletin of the John Rylands University Library
            of Manchester*

BJS   Brown Judaic Studies

BNTC   Black's New Testament Commentaries

BSac   *Bibliotheca Sacra*

BTB	*Biblical Theology Bulletin*
CBET	Contributions to Biblical Exegesis and Theology
CBQ	*The Catholic Biblical Quarterly*
CNT	Commentaire du Nouveau Testament
CRINT	Compendia rerum iudaicarum ad Novum Testamentum
CSEL	Corpus scriptorum ecclesiasticorum latinorum
DicPaul	*Dictionary of Paul and His Letters,* Gerald F. Hawthorne, Ralph P. Martin, and Daniel G. Reid, eds. Downers Grove, Ill./Leicester, U.K.: InterVarsity Press, 1993
EKKNT	Evangelisch-katholischer Kommentar zum Neuen Testament
ET	English translation
EvTh	*Evangelische Theologie*
FRLANT	Forschungen zur Religion und Literatur des Alten und Neuen Testaments
HNT	Handbuch zum Neuen Testament
HTKNT	Herders theologischer Kommentar zum Neuen Testament
HTR	*Harvard Theological Review*
IDBSup	*The Interpreter's Dictionary of the Bible: Supplementary Volume,* K. Crim, ed. Nashville, Tenn.: Abingdon, 1976

Int	*Interpretation*
JBL	*Journal of Biblical Literature*
JSNT	*Journal for the Study of the New Testament*
JSNTSup	Journal for the Study of the New Testament—Supplement Series
JTS	*Journal of Theological Studies*
LD	Lectio divina
LS	*Louvain Studies*
LTPM	Louvain Theological and Pastoral Monographs
LXX	Septuagint
NCBC	The New Century Bible Commentary
NICNT	New International Commentary on the New Testament
NIGTC	The New International Greek Testament Commentary
NJBC	*The New Jerome Bible Commentary*
NovT	*Novum Testamentum*
NovTSup	Novum Testamentum, Supplements
NPNF	A Select Library of the Nicene and Post-Nicene Fathers of the Christian Church, First Series
NTD	Das Neue Testament Deutsch
NTG	Neue Theologische Grundrisse

NTS	*New Testament Studies*
PNTC	The Pelican New Testament Commentaries
PerspRelStud	*Perspectives in Religious Studies*
PL	J. Migne, Patrologia latina
QD	Questiones Disputatae
QL	*Questions liturgiques*
RAug	*Recherches Augustiniennes*
RB	Recherches biblique
RB	*Revue biblique*
RelSRev	*Religious Studies Review*
relstudNews	*religiousstudiesNews*
RNT	Regensburger Neues Testament
SAAHEO	Sancti Aurelii Augustini Hipponensis Episcopi Operum, Maurist ed., 10 vols. + indices. Paris: Franciscus Muguet, 1683–1700
SBLDS	Society of Biblical Literature Dissertation Series
SBLSCS	Society of Biblical Literature Septuagint and Cognate Studies
SBM	Stuttgarter biblische Monographien
SCJ	Studies in Christianity and Judaism
SewTheolRev	*Sewanee Theological Review*
SJT	*Scottish Journal of Theology*

SNTSMS   Society for New Testament Studies Monograph Series

SUNT   Studien zur Umwelt des Neuen Testaments

TDNT   *Theological Dictionary of the New Testament,* 10 vols., Geoffrey W. Bromiley, ed. & trans. (Grand Rapids, Mich./London: Eerdmans, 1964–76)

THKNT   Theologischer Handkommentar zum Neuen Testament

TWNT   *Theologisches Wörterbuch zum Neuen Testament,* 10 vols., Gerhard Kittel, ed. (Stuttgart: W. Kohlhammer, 1933–79)

WBC   Word Biblical Commentary

WEC   Wycliffe Exegetical Commentary

WTJ   *Westminster Theological Journal*

WUNT   Wissenschaftliche Untersuchungen zum Neuen Testament

ZNW   *Zeitschrift für die neutestamentliche Wissenschaft und die Kunde des Urchristentums*

ZTK   *Zeitschrift fur Theologie und Kirche*

Introduction

> "...the Law is holy, and the commandment is holy and just
> and good....the Law is spiritual...." (Rom 7:12, 14).

> "...all who rely on the works of the Law are under a
> curse...." (Gal 3:10).

> "...not having a righteousness of my own that comes from
> the Law, but one that comes through faith in Christ, the
> righteousness from God based on faith...." (Phil 3:9).

In 1986 Joseph Plevnik devoted one chapter of *What Are
They Saying About Paul?*[1] to the topic of justification by faith, a
theme inseparably linked with that of Paul and the Law. Since
then there has been a veritable explosion of writing on the topics
of the Law and justification in Paul; the present work should thus
be considered complementary to the earlier one by Plevnik. It
attempts to contextualize the modern discussion by situating that
discussion in its historical roots as much as possible. It makes no
claim to be exhaustive, though an effort is made to indicate scholars who have treated a major topic in greater detail.

Early in this century William Wrede argued that, in Paul's
view, the Law was an antagonistic force from which human beings
needed to be redeemed, that Paul's rejection of the Law was radical,
and that he differed from Jesus in his view of the Law.[2] More

recently, scholars have strongly questioned such a one-sided inter-pretation. Passages from Paul such as those cited above illustrate that attempting to make sense of Paul's attitude toward the Law is no easy task. In fact, this is perhaps the one thing modern scholarship is agreed upon concerning the topic of Paul and the Law. This situation reflects a major shift in the scholarly discussion of Paul and the Law that has occurred for the most part within the last quarter of the twentieth century. The major catalyst for this change has been the publication of several writings by E. P. Sanders, most notably *Paul and Palestinian Judaism.*[3]

Authors who have followed Sanders in opposing the notion that Paul was arguing against a concept of works-righteousness in the Judaism of his day have come to be described as espousing "The New Perspective on Paul," a characterization based on a 1983 article by J. D. G. Dunn.[4] However, as Donald A. Hagner[5] and C. H. Cosgrove (among others) have pointed out, a number of insights characteristic of the "new perspective" had in fact been espoused by earlier scholars. Cosgrove mentions in particular the work of Dispensationalist scholars such as N. West and A. C. Gaebelein as exhibiting such insights.[6]

The current scholarly discussion about Paul and the Law has its historical roots in the period of the Reformation. In opposition to what he perceived as a misguided reliance on the merits of one's own works in Catholic teaching, Luther went beyond sim-ply arguing that the doctrine of justification by faith alone was central in Paul. The German reformer asserted that justification by faith alone was the principal doctrine of Christianity as well, a touchstone by which all other teachings, works, and forms of worship could be judged. Luther's view sprang from a fundamen-tal pessimism about the ability of human beings to accomplish any kind of good, as well as the accompanying conviction about the necessity for complete reliance on divine mercy.[7]

Before Sanders' challenge, Luther's interpretation of the radi-calism of the opposition between Gospel and Law was the dominant influence in Pauline scholarship, though it was (unsuccessfully) challenged by F. C. Baur of the Tübingen school in the nineteenth century.[8] Even Wrede, who did not believe that Paul's view of the Law was very positive, differed with Luther on the issue of the centrality of the notion of justification by faith, contending that at the center of Pauline theology was a broad perception of redemption: Humanity is enslaved in many ways, and the Law is only one of many oppressive powers from which human beings require deliverance.[9] More recently, Luther's view of the Law has been disputed by, among others, Krister Stendahl, who asserted that the notion that a "legalistic Jew" lurks in the heart of every person distorts the true meaning of Paul.[10]

Because Luther's understanding of the Law/Gospel contrast in Paul was based on his interpretation of the Pauline passages dealing with justification by faith, the precise nature of justification, or righteousness, has been and, for many, continues to be an essential element of the modern debate. Though the scholarly discussion on Law and righteousness in Paul has for the most part been based on the Apostle's letters to the Romans and Galatians, a crucial passage for influential interpretations of the nature of righteousness has been Philippians 3:9: "…and be found in him, not having my own righteousness, that which is from Law, but that which is through faith in Christ, the righteousness from God based upon faith" (my translation).

Two extreme positions regarding the importance of the righteousness terminology in Philippians 3:9 have been espoused in recent scholarship. On the one hand, E. P. Sanders maintains: "The soteriology of the passage…could have been written without the term 'righteousness' at all,"[11] while J. Christiaan Beker asserts that righteousness is the "key term" in Philippians 3:7–11.[12] Interpretations such as those of J. H. Houlden[13] and, more recently, John Reumann[14] likewise give the impression that *righteousness* is the most important term in interpreting the whole of Philippians 3:2–11, though this can be justified neither syntactically nor semantically.[15] The judgment of Sanders probably undergirds the opinion of many authors that the participial construction in Philippians 3:9 is syntactically parenthetical. However, Joachim Gnilka makes a distinction. He considers the construction parenthetical, but nonetheless insists that it expresses an important concept that Paul must have discussed at length with the community previously.[16] Sanders maintains that "righteousness by faith and participation in Christ ultimately amount to the same thing."[17] There is a sense in which this is true, but Peter T. O'Brien has correctly pointed out that while these expressions are synonymous, they are not coterminous.[18]

Virtually all commentators who discuss Philippians 3:9 agree that in this verse two kinds of righteousness are being opposed, namely "my own righteousness, that which is from Law" and "that which is through faith in Christ, the righteousness from God based upon faith." Nonetheless, considerable disagreement exists concerning precisely what is characteristic of each of these two kinds of righteousness. In general, one can suggest three categories that are employed to describe the differences: Human Effort vs. Gift of God, Through Christ vs. not Through Christ, Particular vs. Universal. However, a more fundamental difference is present among these three groups concerning their respective perceptions of the Law. In other areas there is some overlapping. For example, though the second group emphasizes the christological aspect of the righteousness based on faith, this does not imply a denial that such righteousness is a gift of God. Similarly, within the third category, the accent on the universal availability of righteousness based on faith does not exclude either the christological dimension or that of righteousness as a gift of God. Concerning righteousness from Law, authors in the second classification would say that in his discussion of Law Paul argues from solution to plight; those in the first and third divisions would say the argument runs from plight to solution, but would differ on the nature of the plight. Each of the three groups provides a somewhat different answer to the question: "What is wrong with the Law?"

The first group is discussed in chapter 1. Most strongly represented by Rudolf Bultmann and Ernst Käsemann, the scholars in this category would, on the whole, still remain within the tradition of Luther in answering that what is wrong with the Law is that it fosters an attitude of pride which believes that salvation can be accomplished by one's own efforts. Nevertheless, a recent article by P. F. M. Zahl suggests, based on unpublished correspondence between Käsemann and Bultmann from 1927 to 1975, that Käsemann displays remarkable affinity with particular characteristic emphases of the "new perspective."[19]

Scholars in the second group, considered in chapter 2 and championed by E. P. Sanders, would categorically deny the assertion of those in the first classification and reply that what is wrong with the Law is simply that the Law is not Christ. Though some within the second group, notably Sanders, would link this to the notion that the Law is associated with particularism, they differ in general from scholars in the third category in one important respect, the issue of Paul's consistency.

The third group, treated in chapter 3, would likewise deny the major premise of the first and shares the christological perspective of the second but is troubled by the portrait of Paul as hopelessly inconsistent which frequently emerges from the discussion among scholars within the second group. The more nuanced answer of scholars in this third category to the question "What is wrong with the Law?" is that the Law is restrictive in its view of the availability of salvation.

Other scholars who deal with the topic of Law in the letters of Paul have reacted to the work of Sanders by reasserting what they generally refer to as a "Lutheran" position, qualified in various ways. While some of the scholars discussed in the first chapter were already modifying a strict Bultmannian position before the writings of Sanders, those following who still claim to hold a related view are less inclined, in various degrees, to do so in a manner that disparages the Judaism of Paul's day. Sometimes this is consciously expressed; at other times it is implicit in the manner of argumentation. This group is discussed in chapter 4.

In addition to the scholars who fall within these four groups, there are some whose primary question is not so much "What is wrong with the Law, in Paul's view?" but "How can Paul's view of the Law be demonstrated to be coherent and consistent?" Regarding this issue, the scholars in this group, discussed in chapter 5, generally agree with those in the third category above, but they attempt to move the discussion to a wider arena by expanding it beyond Galatians and Romans to include other letters of Paul. For many of the authors within this fifth category, what is wrong with the Law is its connection with sinfulness.

The final chapter deals with the issue of what may be termed the "new center" of Pauline theology. A growing number of scholars contends that the question of the Law is not the central issue in this regard, though as yet there is no consensus as to what should replace it. Some current proposals will be examined in chapter 6, which will conclude with an evaluation of these proposals in view of their relationship to the theme of the Law in the writings of Paul.

1
The Law Fosters an Attitude of Pride

Scholars in the first category, broadly speaking, view the contrast between the two kinds of righteousness discussed by Paul as an opposition between an attitude of (prideful) human effort and humble acceptance of a gift from God. For this group, the most essential (if not the only) thing that is wrong with the Law is that it fosters an attitude of self-aggrandizement and pride which believes that salvation can be accomplished by one's own efforts, though not all these scholars would stress this to the same degree.

The main lines of the position that has become associated with Rudolf Bultmann[1] had been articulated earlier in this century by Karl Barth[2] Wilhelm Michaelis,[3] and Gerhard Friedrich. Friedrich describes the contrast in Philippians 3:9 as being between one's own efforts to fulfill the demands of the Law (as in the case of the Jews alluded to in Rom 10:3) and a gift received through faith.[4] Though a christological focus is not completely absent among the authors who favor this position, the emphasis is primarily on the theological dimension: The "right" kind of righteousness is that which is "from God."

Righteousness as Gift: Rudolf Bultmann

Until fairly recently, Bultmann's view of the characterization of righteousness from Law in Philippians 3:9 was widely held, that is, that the definitive aspect of righteousness from Law in v. 9 is that it is "my own." Linking this expression with the reference to the righteousness of the Jews as "their own" in Romans 10:3, Bultmann concludes that what is wrong with righteousness from Law is that it is based on human effort accompanied by a culpable attitude of prideful boasting in one's own merits; such an attitude is the opposite of humble submissiveness to God. Bultmann then applies this conclusion to all other passages in the letters of Paul that deal with righteousness from Law. In this regard, Bultmann and some of his followers sometimes press the point further than Luther, who distinguished between the Jews and Paul's opponents on the one hand, and the "heretics" of his own day on the other. Luther could at least find understandable the ancient Jewish devotion to the Law because it was given by God.

For his characterization of righteousness based on faith, Bultmann maintains that righteousness is a gift of God because in Philippians 3:9 it is qualified by the prepositional phrase *ek theou* (from God). Bultmann feels that the usage in this passage clarifies the sometimes ambiguous references to *dikaiosynē theou* (righteousness of God) elsewhere in Paul. Based on Philippians 3:9, Bultmann views these other references as also meaning that righteousness is a gift of God.[5] He elsewhere describes that gift of righteousness as forensic (legal) and eschatological (having to do with the end-time),[6] but this description does not depend on Philippians 3:9. Bultmann never attempted a detailed exegesis of Philippians 3:9, and one of the major problems with his interpretation is his failure to read this verse in the light of Philippians 2:12–13, where the Philippian Christians are urged to "work out *your own* salvation…for it is God who is at work in you" (*NRSV,* emphasis mine).

The development of Bultmann's position has come to be referred to as a "Lutheran interpretation," or as a "qualitative argument," because it asserts that there is a fundamentally different way to obtain righteousness, a way other than by means of the Law. Scholars who have held this position include

Jacobus J. Müller, who describes "my" righteousness as that which consists in strict outward fulfillment of the obligations of the Law and which is acquired by virtue of one's own conformity to the Law, while righteousness "from God" is viewed as "imputed."[7] Josef Ernst depicts righteousness from Law as that which is acquired by human effort[8] (as does Ralph P. Martin[9]) and opposes it to the gift that is equivalent to saving righteousness imparted to sinful humanity. D. E. H. Whiteley likewise views the Judaism of Paul's day as reflecting a calculus of merits.[10]

In articles in 1964 and 1979, Günter Klein argues that the key passages for Paul's view of the Law are Galatians 2:16 and Romans 3:20–22, which, he contends, clearly assert that no one is justified by performing works of the Law but only through faith. Klein maintains that Paul's teaching on the Law is determined by his understanding of sin. While it is true that the Law is holy, its purpose is not to afford a means to justification but to reveal sin and incite despair at one's sinfulness in order to move a person to seek righteousness in Christ. Klein strongly maintains that Paul is arguing against the Law in principle, not simply because it is impossible to fulfill.[11]

Hans Hübner, who remarks that his characterization as a follower of Bultmann is only partially true,[12] suggests in his monograph, *Law in Paul's Thought,* that Paul's view developed from a "quantitative" perspective on the Law in Galatians, where he opposed the Law because it was impossible to fully satisfy its requirements (an approach already to be found in the patristic writer John Chrysostom[13]), to a "qualitative" view in Romans, where he argued that the Law was legalistic. The quantitative approach, which has a more christological focus, had earlier been strongly asserted by Ulrich Wilckens, particularly in debate with Klein, in a number of publications.[14] The notion that Paul developed his views between the writing of Galatians and Romans has also been advocated by J. Drane.[15]

Righteousness as New Life: Ernst Käsemann

There have been some scholars who, even before Sanders' thoroughgoing challenge, have concurred with Bultmann up to a point but who have nonetheless strongly critiqued one or another aspect of his interpretation of the characterization of righteousness based on faith. The interpretation of God's righteousness which is generally associated with Ernst Käsemann and his followers had already appeared to some extent in several authors some years before Käsemann's initial presentation of his proposal at the Oxford Congress in September 1961. The connection of righteousness with "the state of forgiveness and the new life" had been asserted by the American James Hardy Ropes of Cambridge, Massachusetts, as early as 1903.[16] In 1951, the British scholar F. C. Synge, writing in a commentary series aimed at the "intelligent general reader," offered an interpretation of "righteousness from God" in Philippians 3:9 that accepts Bultmann's notion of the gift character of righteousness and includes an acknowledgment of its eschatological dimension but totally disagrees with the depiction of this gift as forensic.[17] Synge regards it rather as having to do with God's saving and judging activity which takes place in Christ and which is experienced by human beings as regeneration or re-creation.[18] A number of the qualities associated with righteousness by Käsemann had also previously been remarked on by the Belgian exegete Lucien Cerfaux.[19]

In his 1959 commentary on Philippians, Francis Wright Beare agrees with the emphasis of Bultmann on "prideful achievement"[20] as characteristic of "my own righteousness, that from Law" and accepts both the gift character and the forensic dimension of "righteousness from God." Nonetheless, he perceives a difficulty in understanding Paul's righteousness language both in Philippians 3:9 and in general because, Beare feels, Paul employs the term *righteousness* in two different senses. "My own righteousness, from Law" has to do with a level of moral achievement, a conduct and character of which God as judge will approve. However, Beare is of the opinion that Paul has somewhat forced an "unnatural" forensic sense onto the "righteousness from God" terminology: "'Forensic' language cannot be used without strain in the context of divine dealings with man which are expressly put under the rubric 'apart from Law' (Rom iii. 21)."[21] For Beare the fundamental meaning of "righteousness from God" is "forgiveness of sins," though this does not exclude the aspect of God's judgment. In addition, "righteousness from God" has the dimension of the victorious power of God that triumphs over evil and initiates the kingdom of peace on earth, in anticipation of the total eschatological victory of the end-time. It is imparted to the believer in such a way as to take command of the believer's life, as triumph over unrighteousness and sin.[22] Thus, though being willing to accept a forensic sense in Paul's concept of "righteousness from God," Beare does not feel that this is the sense proper to this concept, and certainly not the only sense.

While Käsemann is generally perceived as holding a position opposite to that of Bultmann on the meaning of "righteousness from God," he basically agrees with Bultmann on the broad outlines of the interpretation of Philippians 3:9, that is, that the opposition in Philippians 3:9 is between righteousness acquired by human effort and righteousness coming from God as a gift. Käsemann, however, disagrees with Bultmann's characterization of the gift as "forensic-eschatological," maintaining that the gift should be associated with the saving power of God. This contention, however, is not based on Philippians 3:9 (a passage to which Käsemann devoted even less attention than Bultmann) but on an examination of biblical and Qumran material interwoven with references to (mostly) Romans, Galatians, and the Corinthian correspondence.[23] Within this discussion, Käsemann begins by asserting that the primary emphasis is on the power of God that acts effectively to accomplish salvation.[24] Justification cannot be separated from sanctification.[25] It has much more to do with relationships than with a personal ethical quality.[26] It means, for the Christian, becoming a new creation because one experiences a change of lordship.[27] The idea of new creation which

Käsemann derives from the Adam-Christ passages had been noted earlier by Cerfaux, who also stressed the gift quality of righteousness.[28]

Scholars such as Manfred T. Brauch incline toward Käsemann's interpretation of righteousness,[29] while Günter Klein is representative of those who are quite critical of many of the points argued by Käsemann.[30] Klein in turn has been criticized for the "arbitrariness" of his exegesis of Romans 3 by Richard B. Hays. Hays nevertheless believes that the attempts of Käsemann to find support for his interpretation of righteousness in Qumran parallels and the subsequent efforts of his students to demonstrate some type of apocalyptic foundation for Paul's use of "righteousness of God" terminology have not been persuasive. However, Hays is convinced of the correctness of Käsemann's insight that "righteousness of God" for Paul is God's salvation-creating power. Hays endeavors to establish this assertion based on an examination of the internal logic of Paul's argument in Romans 3 and of Psalm 143 as background for that argument.[31]

Nils Alstrup Dahl (1982),[32] Jouette M. Bassler, (1982)[33] David Hall (1983),[34] and C. H. Cosgrove (1987)[35] all accept that Paul's concept of "righteousness of God" in Romans 3 includes the idea of God's saving power, in addition stressing somewhat more than Hays does that God's righteousness as saving power includes the idea of God exercising judgment. John W. Olley asserts the overlapping of these two notions in the Septuagint notion of righteousness.[36]

Ralph P. Martin (in the revised edition of his commentary on Philippians, 1980) is representative of exegetes who attempt to combine the insights of Bultmann and Käsemann in interpreting the meaning of "righteousness from God" in Philippians 3:9. Martin regards the association between "being found in Christ" and "having righteousness" from a perspective which views the "juridical flavor" of "being found" in Philippians 3:9 as coming from the righteousness terminology that follows.[37] He apparently assumes that righteousness terminology is primarily forensic, though agreeing with John A. Ziesler (see next section below) that the righteousness referred to in Philippians 3:9 is "forensic and ethical at once." In addition, though Martin believes that in this verse Paul explains his teaching on an individualistic basis, Martin does accept a more cosmic dimension having to do with the idea of a new creation (following in the line of Käsemann) insofar as Paul's more general teaching on righteousness is concerned.[38] J. Christiaan Beker also blends elements from both Bultmann and Käsemann,[39] as does Brendan Byrne, who regards "both sides [Bultmann and Käsemann] as indicating essential aspects of Paul's concept of God's 'righteousness.'"[40]

Righteousness as Participation: Stuhlmacher and Ziesler

Peter Stuhlmacher, a student of Käsemann, in a monograph on righteousness in Paul (1965),[41] views the opposition between the two kinds of righteousness in Philippians 3:9 as having to do with Paul's perception of the Law before and after baptism.[42] Before baptism Paul could think of the Law as a "Law of life" (Sir 17:11); after baptism, he anticipated God's judgment only "in Christ." Following in the line of Käsemann (though apparently with some openness to Bultmann's nuance of "forensic-eschatological" righteousness), Stuhlmacher insists that righteousness from God is not only an eschatological-forensic valuation, but also (and perhaps more importantly) the experience of a new condition, another way of describing the same reality elsewhere portrayed as the conferring of the Spirit. This new condition is a participation in the death and the victory of Christ (Phil 3:10) and is thus an experience of God's saving victory, which is the same as God's creative activity, the saving justice described in Isaiah 54:17.

John A. Ziesler, in a 1972 work, seems to accept without much discussion Bultmann's understanding of one's "own" righteousness as something having to do with human achievement,[43] although this aspect of Ziesler's position is strongly modified in his discussion of Philippians 3:9 and in two more recent works, primarily as a result of the influence of Sanders.[44] In *The Meaning of Righteousness in Paul,* Ziesler begins by asserting that the syntactic relation of the participial construction in Philippians 3:9 is that of subordination to "be found in him," and that therefore the participatory dimension is primary. Ziesler uses *participation* language vis-à-vis *forensic* where formerly the distinction was more often between *mystical* and *juridical* terminology in Paul. Many scholars[45] have repeated, without much or any amplification, the brief remark of Martin Dibelius[46] that mystical and juridical thought are not easily separable in Paul. Joachim Gnilka suggests replacing the term *mystical* with *pneumatisch* (spiritual),[47] implicitly recognizing that part of the difficulty with *mystical* is that commentators who use this term often do so without defining precisely what they mean by it. Friedrich contrasts *ethisch-juridische* and *physisch-mystische;*[48] some authors oppose *ethical* and *juridical,* and yet both of these terms have been linked with *relational.* Georg Strecker has proposed *ontological* as an alternative to *mystical.*[49] In recent discussion *mystical* has largely been replaced by *participation(ist)* and *forensic* is somewhat more common than *juridical.*

Thus, according to Ziesler, the believer does not *possess* righteousness, but *participates* in it by faith; it remains God's righteousness. Insofar as the believer is concerned, this righteousness exists only in and through the relationship with Christ and is closely linked to dying and rising with Christ. Ziesler is unwilling to accept Beare's definition of righteousness from God as forgiveness because he believes that with such an understanding Paul's opposition of the two kinds of righteousness would not make sense. If righteousness by Law is taken in its usual sense of moral achievement,[50] while righteousness by faith is forgiveness,[51] the second type "not only has a different origin, it is a different species. The first is behavioural (though with overtones of relationship and acceptability), but the second is to do with relationship and acceptability with no behavioural overtones at all."[52] Ziesler rejects Beare's premise that Paul is using righteousness terminology in two different senses and contends that *acceptability* as a meaning for *righteousness* is not supported in other literature.[53] Ziesler then briefly considers the possibility that Paul refers to the rabbinic doctrine of merits and concludes that while this doctrine may be in the background in Romans 4 and Galatians 3, the indications of its presence there (e.g., the use of the verb *logizomai*) are not apparent in Philippians 3.[54] One might perhaps question whether the disparity that Ziesler perceives in Beare is really such a problem, since, for example, in Philippians 2:12–13 Paul can write: "…work out your own salvation with fear and trembling; for it is God who is at work in you, enabling you both to will and to work for his good pleasure" (NRSV). Clearly here the behavioral aspect flows from a relationship that is dependent on the divine initiative, yet it is also necessary as a response to this initiative.

While Ziesler does detect some overtones of a forensic nature in the context of Philippians 3:7–11,[55] he insists that this context does not allow limiting the meaning of righteousness in this passage to the forensic dimension. The implication of new existence in Christ, the references to dying and rising with Christ and knowing the power of his resurrection would not be necessary, Ziesler asserts, if the point being emphasized is simply the imputation of righteousness. Being in Christ implies a radical and ethical newness. *Ethical* is apparently to be understood in the context of the exhortations present in Philippians 2:1–13 and the allusion to the "fruits of righteousness" in 1:11. Righteousness, then, is fully ethical and is communicated to us insofar as we have faith in Jesus. This communication is not a transfer of something from God to human beings, but (primarily) a participation by believers in God's righteousness (by which Ziesler does not seem to mean an attribute of God but rather a creation of God and a gift of God)[56] through Christ. It also has forensic or relational implications, but they cannot be considered exhaustive of its meaning. For Ziesler in the *dikai-* word group, the verb is essentially relational or forensic, and the noun and adjective describe behavior within a relationship.[57] In discussing the biblical concept of righteousness, Ziesler maintains that righteousness generally means acting loyally within the covenant relationship. Nonetheless, *ethical* and *forensic* are inseparable, for those who act loyally "are in a state of loyalty and will be adjudged thus....A verdict about guilt or innocence was really a verdict about loyalty or disloyalty, for both human and divine justice."[58] Thus when Judah says of Tamar (Gen 38:26), "She is more righteous than I," he probably means not simply that she is more in the right, but also, and perhaps more importantly, "She has fulfilled the community obligations better than I have."[59]

In his review of Ziesler's monograph, Nigel M. Watson accepts this interpretation of righteousness in Philippians 3:9.[60] In general, Watson commends Ziesler for differentiating between Paul's use of the verb on the one hand and the noun and adjective on the other in discussing righteousness terminology, though Watson is of the opinion that there is more overlapping in these two areas than Ziesler finds. Watson feels the most important point Ziesler's study makes is that God's saving righteousness on behalf of human beings accomplishes two things inseparably: "...it restores their relationship with God and it makes them new (ethical, righteous) beings."[61] In view of this remark, one could question whether the notion of restoring a relationship with God excludes the concept of forgiveness, as Ziesler contends in his critique of Beare.[62]

The Law and Sacred Violence: R. G. Hamerton-Kelly

R. G. Hamerton-Kelly has perhaps taken the Bultmannian position to the greatest possible extreme in a section of his 1992 monograph *Sacred Violence: Paul's Hermeneutic of the Cross* (1992),[63] as well as an article the following year.[64] Using René Girard's theory of sacred violence, Hamerton-Kelly contends that the reason Paul repudiated the Law is that he came to view it as an entity which represented and served religion as a structure of sacred violence. A number of scholars have taken issue with this view from various perspectives.[65]

In distinction from Hamerton-Kelly, Neil Elliott, in a 1993 article, contends that from his new perspective, that of the cross of Christ, Paul came to regard only one specific political configuration of Judaism as connected with sacred violence. This one instance was connected with the "jockeying for power of the Judean Temple state." Elliott also maintains that Paul came to recognize that same violence in his own persecution of Jewish Christians.[66]

The methodology resulting from Hamerton-Kelly's utilization of Girard's theories is severely criticized in a review of Hamerton-Kelly's book by Stanley B. Marrow:

> Judging by the conclusion of the book, the chapters... "Sacred Violence and the Jews" and "Sacred Violence and the Law of Moses" are, in a sense, the raison d'être of the work as a whole. Here, as perhaps nowhere in the preceding chapters, it becomes evident that the new things said are not quite true and cannot be made so by being sired upon René Girard, and that the true things proffered are not quite new and do not owe what truth they possess to Girardian theory....the Girardian theory, instead of being an obedient tool of elucidation, has become a tyrannous master of obfuscation....[67]

Summary

While the interpretations discussed in this chapter differ in greater or lesser degree on the meaning of the "righteousness from God" alluded to in Philippians 3:9, they generally assume that "my own righteousness, that based on Law" in that passage, as well as "their own righteousness" in Romans 10:3, refers to legalistic moral achievement, something accomplished by human effort and in which human beings can and do take pride. Thus, the first of the two negative characterizations in Philippians 3:9 defines the second, that is, what is wrong with righteousness from Law is that it is "mine." The Law is viewed as fostering an attitude that leads not only to boasting, but also even to violence.

The scholars in the next group to be discussed have totally rejected Bultmann's contention that "my own righteousness" (Phil 3:9) and "their own righteousness" (Rom 10:3) depict an attitude of prideful reliance on one's own efforts. They maintain that there is no evidence anywhere in Paul to support such a conclusion.

2
The Law Is Not Christ

Among the scholars who advocate "the new perspective on Paul," the position that in Paul's view there is nothing inherently wrong with the Law is coupled with a positive appreciation of Judaism. From this perspective, Bultmann's negative opinion of Law is regarded as having resulted from an incorrect understanding of Jewish doctrine and practice in the early Christian period. Within this group, the opposition between the two kinds of righteousness in Philippians 3:9 is based on the fact that one type of righteousness comes through Christ and the other does not. In Paul's thought as a whole, as well as in Philippians 3:9 in particular, the opinion of these scholars can be summed up in the statement of E. P. Sanders: "What is wrong with Israel's righteousness by Law…is that it is not based on faith in Christ…and that it prevents Gentiles from being on equal footing with Jews."[1]

Anticipations of E. P. Sanders

F. C. Synge, who anticipated some of the remarks of Käsemann in regard to "righteousness from God" in 1951, likewise seems to have been one of the first authors to describe the meaning of "my own righteousness" in Philippians 3:9 in terms that today are most commonly associated with E. P. Sanders. While Synge begins by paraphrasing the meaning of "my own righteousness" as "such obedience to the Law of God that one could claim to be in the right with God,"[2] he goes on to make some qualifications. He notes, with reference to Psalm 119 and Job 31, that "righteousness after the Law" was uprightness of a very high order and that the Pharisees were good people who only exceptionally might have had a self-congratulatory attitude regarding their own virtue. Most of them would have accepted that complete righteousness was not attainable through keeping the Law and would have relied on the mercy of God to supplement this righteousness from Law with righteousness that was a gift from God. The difference Synge sees in Paul's perspective is that the gift of righteousness from God is no longer considered supplemental, but a re-creation that is experienced already in the present because in Christ the kingdom of God has come.[3] Thus, the distinction between "my own righteousness, from Law" and "the righteousness from God which comes through faith in Christ" seems to be for Synge more a matter of degree. Righteousness from Law is rejected by Paul not because it has to do with prideful human effort, but simply because it is incomplete. It is not so much rejected as supplanted.

This implied suggestion that the Jewish Law had been superseded was already explicitly stated in a medieval commentary attributed to Lanfranc.[4] As will be evident elsewhere in this discussion, one can look still earlier to Augustine for similar comments. At the beginning of Book 32 of *Contra Faustum* (composed 397–98), Augustine cites Faustus' charge that his opponents, including Augustine, selectively accept some parts of the Jewish Scripture, but consider the rest in the same way that Paul thought of those things that he considered *stercora* (garbage; the Greek term in Phil 3:8 is *skybala*). Augustine replies that those things from Jewish Scripture that are no longer observed are not disdained. Rather, they are considered to have been suitable to their time and people; in addition, they are still symbolic of spiritual truths. Though their outward observance has been abolished, they are to be respected as prophecy and shadow of things to come.[5]

Another early challenge to the slanted view of first-century Judaism long prevalent in Pauline scholarship was that of the Jewish scholar H. J. Schoeps (1961), who essentially argues that Paul, along with other Jewish rabbis of his day, believed that the coming of the Messiah would put an end to the demands of the Law. However, Schoeps charges Paul with the blame for a distorted view of the Judaism of his day, believing that Paul's acceptance of Jesus as Messiah led him to an interpretation of the Law that would not have been accepted by his Jewish contemporaries and that in effect was a misconstrual because it separated the Law from the covenant.[6]

The position that in Philippians 3:9 the Law is being seen as having been superseded as a means of salvation was also espoused by Andrea van Dülmen in her 1968 monograph on Paul's theology of the Law[7] and in an article by Ulrich Wilckens[8] the same year. Van Dülmen, a Roman Catholic, espouses many of the arguments traditionally associated with a "Lutheran" position; both authors contend that Paul's basic criticism of the Law is christological. Wilckens comments that in both Philippians 3:9 and Romans 10:3 the Law has become an "anachronism" insofar as saving history is concerned. He takes as his point of departure Romans 2:13 and, unlike most scholars, maintains that Paul means exactly what he says, that the doers of the Law will be justified. The problem is that it is impossible to fulfill the Law in its entirety. Nonetheless, Christian faith is not opposed to works, nor does faith excuse the believer from the obligation to fulfill the Law. Faith brings deliverance from the consequences of past sin as well as from inadequacy in living up to the Law in the present. Because all have sinned, the Law has already become inoperative as a means of life, having been replaced by God's saving act of righteousness in Christ. However, the Law remains as a statement of God's will, and believers are obliged to fulfill it.[9]

Two Kinds of Righteousness: E. P. Sanders

Sanders, in *Paul and Palestinian Judaism,* argues that it is not the means, that is, the activity of doing the Law, that is wrong as such, but rather that this means leads to the wrong end (righteousness based on the Law rather than salvation in Christ).[10] While not the first to make this assertion, Sanders provides extensive documentation in attempting to counter the underlying presumption of Bultmann's interpretation, the presumption that first-century Judaism was a religion of legalistic works-righteousness.

Sanders makes Philippians 3:9 a key to his perception of righteousness as a "transfer term" in Paul. Sanders thus perceives the problem raised by Beare (though apparently independently of Beare) that Paul seems to be using righteousness terminology in two different senses in Philippians 3:9. He argues that just as Philippians 3:2–3 contrasts a true and false circumcision, so 3:9 opposes a true and false righteousness, and that in making this contrast Paul was aware of his own transfer in the meaning of the term *righteousness.*[11]

In view of this, Sanders asserts, all the passages in Romans and Galatians that state that righteousness does not come by works of Law should be interpreted to mean that the *right kind of righteousness* cannot come by works of Law, but comes only through Christ.[12] Sanders maintains that righteousness by faith ultimately amounts to participation in Christ,[13] though Paul "does not use the righteousness terminology with *any one* meaning."[14] This is a modification of an earlier position, expressed in "Patterns of Religion in Paul and Rabbinic Judaism," where Sanders had contended (as Moisés Silva has also suggested more recently) that the "real" meaning of righteousness for Paul is "life."[15] The modification in Sanders' position is the result of dialogue with Ziesler.

Sanders argues against the view that "my righteousness, based on Law" in Philippians 3:9 refers to merit achieved based on performance of good deeds, which inherently leads to boasting.[16] Such a view, he maintains, requires a conflation of Philippians 3:9

with Romans 3:27 and 4:2 as well as the understanding of *boasting* as "boasting in one's individual performance" rather than in the special status of Israel. In addition, this view requires two assumptions which Paul does not express, namely: (1) righteousness by Law is meritorious achievement that gives one the right to claim a reward from God, and is thus a denial of grace; (2) righteousness by Law is self-evidently a bad thing. Further, one must assume that Paul accused Judaism of leading to this state of affairs.

Sanders admits that there may appear to be some ground for the conflation of Philippians 3:3–11 with Romans 3:27 and 4:2 because of the mention of "confidence in the flesh" in Philippians 3:3 as well as the assertion of Paul that this confidence was partly in status and partly in accomplishment. This can seem to suggest that Paul accused Judaism, in the person of his former self, of the attitude of boastful self-righteousness.[17] This impression may appear to be further confirmed if it is presupposed that Jewish literature itself manifests Judaism to be a religion of legalistic self-righteousness, a view against which Sanders also contends strongly in *Paul and Palestinian Judaism.*[18] This view also assumes that Paul "must have" expressed an opposition to self-righteousness because such an opposition is part of Christian faith. However, according to Sanders, the text of Philippians 3:9 within its context does not support such an interpretation: "Paul does not say that boasting in status and achievement was wrong because boasting is the wrong attitude, but that he boasted in things that *were gain.* They *became loss* because, in his black and white world, there is no second best."[19] Paul's criticism of his former life is not that he had a self-righteous attitude, but that he put confidence in something other than Christ. Thus, Sanders concludes, "my own righteousness" in Philippians 3:9 *is* the same as "their own righteousness" in Romans 10:3; in both cases it is the peculiar result of being an observant Jew. In and of itself this is a good thing, but it is shown to be wrong by the revelation of "God's righteousness," which comes by faith in Christ.[20]

Sanders' argument is further strengthened if it is noted that Paul does not actually say in Philippians 3:3–6 that he "boasted" *(kauchaomai)* in his prerogatives of birth and zeal, but that he had more reason than his opponents to "rely" *(pepoithēsis)* on them. The Greek word translated "boasting" includes the notion of relying on, but to such a degree that one boasts, or glories in, whatever one relies on.[21] "Relying on flesh," though not to be condoned, does not *necessarily* signify an attitude of boasting, much less of arrogance.

Christ the End of the Law: Schenk, Badenas, Wright, Bechtler, Edgar, Moo, Fitzmyer

The German exegete Wolfgang Schenk, in his commentary on Philippians (1984), argues along lines similar to those of Sanders. Schenk demonstrates that the zeal which Paul ascribes to himself in Philippians 3:6 need not be taken in a negative sense. He points out that *zeal* is linguistically related to the imperative *stēkete* (stand [firm]) in Philippians 4:1 and might possibly be taken synonymously. He refers to Sirach 45:23, where the zeal of Phineas is related to his "standing firm," and to Numbers 25:10–13, where the zeal (v. 13) of Phineas is praised because he made atonement for Israel and thus caused the zeal of God (= the punishing judgment of God) to cease. In Psalm 105:30–31, the fact that Phineas "stood up" is reckoned to him as righteousness, and in Wisdom 5:17–18, God's zeal is associated with God's righteousness. In Romans 10:2, the zeal of Israel is conceded; it is not associated with arrogance but is said to rest on a false basis because it is without knowledge.[22] The self-presentation of Paul in Philippians 3:4–6 can be compared formally to that of Jewish wisdom teachers described in Romans 2:17–19; however, the main point Paul is stressing is not the sinfulness of the Jews, though Schenk does not deny there is some element of this in Romans 2, but rather the new initiative of God's grace. The ultimate goal of the argumentation in Romans is that Christ is the new Adam, not the new Moses. The Sinai covenant has become anachronistic after Easter because in the resurrection God has begun a new creation. If Christ had not risen, the way of the synagogue would in fact be the unique way that has been pointed out (by God).[23]

In another section,[24] Schenk notes the difference between the prepositions that govern the word *righteousness* in Philippians 3:6 and 3:9. In 3:6, Paul speaks of righteousness *in* the Law, while 3:9 refers to righteousness *from* (in the sense of *based on*) Law. The *en nomo* (in Law) of 3:6 is linked with the *en sarki* (in flesh) of 3:3, but it would be incorrect to perceive a concept of "works-righteousness" in 3:6, since the Qumran documents give evidence that a perception of being righteous does not exclude an awareness of sin, a point made earlier by Robert Gundry.[25] While Schenk relies heavily on Sanders, he additionally comments on agreement with many of the assertions made by Sanders in other (German) authors such as Jürgen Becker,[26] Herbert Braun,[27] and Joachim Schüpphaus.[28] Schenk agrees with Sanders[29] that Philippians 3:9 has a parenthetical character: It has been imported into a passage that is primarily soteriological and stated in participationist terms because of the attacks of the people in 3:2 and their apparent claim that they and not the Christians[30] are the true circumcision.[31] In general, though he brings in some further documentation to support the argumentation, Schenk's position on Philippians 3:9 is that of Sanders: What is being contrasted in Philippians 3:9 is not human effort and God's grace, but a kind of righteousness that comes through Christ and one that does not. What is wrong with the Law is not that it fosters prideful self-achievement, but simply that it has been supplanted.

From a slightly different perspective, Robert Badenas (1985), after an extensive study of the meaning and history of *telos,* concludes that, because of the more prevalent meaning of *telos* as "goal" and because of the athletic imagery in the immediate context of Romans 9:30–33, "goal" is a preferable meaning to "termination" for Paul's reference to Christ as the "end" of the

Law in Romans 10:4. Thus, *nomos* (Law) here refers to divine revelation rather than to an ethical code.[32]

N. T. Wright (1992) has likewise argued that Paul's statements about Christ and the Law reflect the apostle's belief that the covenant purposes of the God of Israel attained their climactic point in the death and resurrection of Jesus.[33] A similar emphasis is found in a recent article (1994) by Steven Richard Bechtler, who maintains that in Romans 10:4 Paul identifies Christ as the goal toward which God intended that Torah should lead Israel, not as the end, in the sense of termination, of Torah. Bechtler stresses that the fault of Israel does not consist in a prideful attitude of works righteousness, but rather in a failure to understand that Torah is meant to lead to Christ. Rejection of Christ thus signifies nonattainment of Torah.[34] That the Law is an instrument that points to Christ is also the contention of C. F. Edgar (1996). He examines Paul's view on the function of the Law as expressed in Romans 9:30—10:4, using the methodology of narrative dimension, and concludes that from this perspective Paul's view of the Law as an instrument pointing to Christ is consistent with that of the Pentateuch.[35]

While many scholars take an either/or position on whether *telos* in Romans 10:4 means "goal" or "termination," some prefer to combine the two meanings. Douglas Moo (1987), after surveying a number of earlier approaches to the question of the meaning of *telos* in Romans 10:4, concludes: "To argue that Paul is claiming Christ as the ultimate goal of the Law, and that, having attained its goal, the Law is in some important manner no longer applicable, may very well do justice both to exegetical considerations and to the larger picture of the Law in Paul."[36] Joseph A. Fitzmyer (1993), who prefers the meaning "goal," briefly lists the authors who hold these respective positions in the discussion of Romans 10:4 in his commentary on Romans.[37]

Renunciation of Covenant Status:
Räisänen, Ziesler, F. Watson

The Finnish scholar Heikki Räisänen follows in the line of Sanders in rejecting the notion that "my righteousness, that which is from Law" in Philippians 3:9 has to do with human achievement. In a 1980 article, Räisänen argues against Bultmann's "human achievement" interpretation in a discussion of all the relevant passages and concludes:

> Paul does not condemn [in Phil 3:9] his previous blamelessness. He only brands it as blamelessness "according to the Law" and as "his own righteousness, coming from the Law," which is nothing in comparison with the union with Christ. This is analogous to the juxtaposition of vanishing and permanent glory as depicted in 2 Cor 3....The Jews err in imagining that they can be saved by keeping the Law rather than believing in Christ; the root of the evil lies in a christological failure, not in an anthropological one....Paul may have seen some tendency toward smugness and self-righteousness in the Jewish way. But this was a by-product, not the underlying basic error.[38]

Räisänen takes a similar position a few years later in his book *Paul and the Law* (1983).[39] In a 1987 article, he points out that the first four of the "fleshly" advantages that Paul lists in Philippians 3:4–6 were not of Paul's own doing.[40] Räisänen further notes that the language of "blamelessness" need not evidence a spirit of pride in one's own efforts. Rather, it functions in the same way as in the description of Zachary and Elizabeth in Luke 1:6, that is, it describes a pious person obediently fulfilling duties prescribed by the Law of God.[41] Elsewhere, however, Räisänen expresses the view that Philippians 3:6 asserts that Paul kept the Law "perfectly."[42] E. P. Sanders also seems at one point to hold such an opinion,[43] though he somewhat qualifies this: "...at least for rhetorical purposes, Paul could entertain the possibility of human blamelessness."[44]

Philippians 3:4–8, according to Räisänen, shows that from the time of his initial encounter with Christ Paul perceived that whatever separated Jews from Gentiles was loss rather than gain. However, he believes that v. 9, which is often asserted to be the ground of the antithesis (between justification by works of Law and justification by faith) in Paul's conversion experience,[45] may be rather an interpretation of Paul's experience in retrospect. The "parenthetical" character of v. 9, where an interpretation couched in *juridical* vocabulary interrupts a description of Christian existence portrayed in *participationist* terms, suggests this.[46] Thus, "Verse 9 may well introduce second thoughts on the significance of the Damascus experience."[47]

Räisänen does not immediately develop the suggestion that v. 9 might be retrospective, but goes on at this point to consider the train of thought in v. 9. He senses a strain in the contrast between the two kinds of righteousness and maintains that "What Paul renounces according to Philippians 3:7ff. is his whole covenant-status as a Jew, which includes reliance on the divine gifts bestowed uniquely on Israel as well as the confirmation of those gifts by his own obedience."[48]

The view that in Philippians 3:7ff. Paul is renouncing his covenant-status as a Jew in its entirety is also held by Francis Watson (1986),[49] who approaches the issue from a different perspective; he contends that "the starting point for interpreting Paul's statements about Judaism, the law, and the Gentiles must be sociological rather than theological. If one presupposes that the law was a problem for Paul primarily for theological and existential reasons, one will misunderstand what he has to say on the subject."[50]

Räisänen maintains that while in this passage Paul, in effect, renounces the biblical covenant, "he cannot admit that this is what his actual position implies." According to Räisänen, in both Romans 9—10 and Philippians 3:9, Paul is struggling with an impossible task in attempting to hold together two incompatible convictions: that God has made an irrevocable covenant with

Israel and given Israel God's Law, which invites to righteous life, but at the same time that this righteousness is not true righteousness, since it is not based on faith in Jesus.[51]

Though Sanders has also asserted this alleged contradiction,[52] Räisänen has expressed in several places the opinion that Sanders has not gone far enough. In "Legalism and Salvation" (1981) Räisänen comments that Sanders' remark, "Paul did not so much misunderstand the role of the Law in Judaism as gain a new perspective which led him to dethrone the Law,"[53] is correct, but leaves unanswered the question of why Paul misrepresented the Law.[54] In *Paul and the Law* (1983), Räisänen concludes that Paul had, by way of intuition, or because of his faith in Christ, come to important insights regarding such things as the Christian's freedom, but that he was never able to give a logical explanation for these insights.[55] In "Paul's Conversion" (1987), Räisänen is somewhat more positive. Based on his assumption that Philippians 3:9 may reflect an idea that was not present in Paul's mind at the time of his conversion,[56] Räisänen goes on in the rest of this article to suggest that Paul's dissatisfaction with the Law developed gradually under the influence of polemic and that the position he eventually adopted was that of the Hellenists.[57]

In his 1989 commentary on Romans, Ziesler makes clear his agreement with Sanders that in Romans "Paul's target is not human and in particular Jewish self-righteousness."[58] In a comparatively lengthy section of the introduction,[59] Ziesler presents in overview form the results of the exegesis worked out in detail in his commentary regarding the place of the Law in the thought of Paul's Letter to the Romans. He gives primacy to this letter itself as the best context for understanding individual passages about righteousness and the Law, making every effort to determine which of the various meanings translated by the Greek word *nomos* (Torah, Law, principle [which for Ziesler could include the meaning of régime]) makes best sense in an individual passage.

Prescinding from Galatians, Ziesler maintains that the Letter to the Romans offers two reasons for negative statements about the Law: (1) If acceptance into the people of God is equally available to Gentiles and Jews on the grounds of faith, then circumcision no longer provides such grounds, and since circumcision is the sign of life under the Torah, Torah-obedience can no longer be viewed as the distinguishing mark of the people of God. (2) Faith in Jesus Christ as the criterion of righteousness excludes every other criterion, including Torah-obedience. Israel was called to be the people of God, but this was always more a matter of call and promise than of keeping the Law. Nonetheless, it is also clear that Paul believed Christians were obliged to *live* as God's people: "...although the written Torah as such and as a whole is not binding on Christians, the fundamental will of God certainly is, and this includes such things as the Law against coveting and the command to love."[60] "In sum," Ziesler concludes,

> Paul's statements about the Law are problematic and difficult to reconcile with one another. It would be rash to claim that the interpretation offered here does away with all the difficulties; perhaps no interpretation is likely to do that, and we may be forgiven for suspecting that Paul had not managed to sort the whole matter out for himself. Nevertheless the contention now being made is that in Romans Paul does reject the Torah both as a means to salvation, and also as the definitive guide to life under God, more radically and more consistently than is sometimes allowed.[61]

While the proponents of a "christological" explanation of Philippians 3:9 have succeeded in pointing out both the error of assuming a "works-righteousness" as universally characteristic of first-century Judaism and the lack of textual support to assume that Paul was referring to such a notion in Philippians 3:9, the christological explanation does not solve all the problems of interpretation, as Ziesler has acknowledged. Francis Watson's solution to the question "What is wrong with the Law?" is that all Paul's theoretical discussions of themes such as Law, works, grace, and faith should be regarded as an attempt to legitimate the social reality of sectarian Gentile Christian communities in which the Law was not observed.[62] Paul first preached to the Jews and, being unsuccessful, turned to the Gentiles. To make it easier for them to accept Christianity, he abrogated Jewish laws.[63] If one wishes to demonstrate consistency in Paul's statements about the Law, therefore, it must be sought "not primarily at the theoretical level but at the level of practical strategy."[64] In contrast to Sanders, Watson asserts that though it was Paul who enabled Christianity to transform itself into a world religion, thus attaining universality, this was not what Paul intended: "If in one sense it is true that Paul sought to break down the barrier between Jew and Gentile, he nevertheless did so only to reestablish exclusiveness in a new form."[65]

A major problem regarding Watson's thesis is that it does not explain why Paul turned to Christianity in the first place, a question that seemingly needs to be answered from a theological perspective. A number of scholars have been critical of various points of Watson's presentation. W. S. Campbell, in a 1989 article, questions whether Paul really advocated separation from the synagogue.[66] Thomas R. Schreiner has criticized Watson's perspective as flawed

> ...because it too neatly separates theology from sociology. It is too simplistic to conclude that social factors *alone* were the decisive reasons for Paul's viewpoint on the Law and the Jew-Gentile issue. This is an example of reductionist reasoning....Despite Watson's disclaimer to the effect that he is not eliminating Paul the theologian, Paul's theology is relegated to an insignificant level in his study. Pauline arguments for inclusion of Gentiles are simply rationalizations for what he wanted to prove in the first place, according to Watson....The inclusion of Gentiles into the people of God cannot be separated from Paul's claim that righteousness does not come by observing the Law. The two issues belong together and cannot be separated without doing violence to Paul's writings.[67]

Schreiner has criticized Michael Winger's 1992 study, which utilizes the methodology of lexical semantics to determine the meaning of *nomos* in Paul's letters,[68] on similar grounds, noting that Winger consistently minimizes the divine origin of the Law for Paul, in effect, reducing the Law to sociological categories and virtually eliminating the theological dimension of *nomos* in Paul.[69]

The Theological Value of Galatians: Frank J. Matera

In the introduction to his 1992 commentary on the Letter to the Galatians,[70] as well as at pertinent locations within the more detailed treatment, Frank Matera discusses the question of Paul's view of the Law specifically in Galatians. He begins by asserting that Galatians is more about doing the right works of the Law and appropriate cultural behavior in order to become a full member of Israel than about legalism, righteousness, and personal salvation.[71] With reference to Stendahl, Sanders, Dunn, and F. Watson, Matera reiterates that the question of Galatians is "what are the entrance requirements for Gentile Christians who want to be recognized as full members of that portion of Israel which believes in Jesus the Messiah?" Is it mandatory to accept circumcision, practice specific dietary regulations, and follow the Jewish religious calendar, or "is it possible to be accepted as a full member of the Church on the basis of faith in Christ, apart from doing these works of the Mosaic Law?"[72]

Matera concedes that "Judaism, like every religion, has its legalistic side,"[73] but insists on the inaccuracy of the perception of first-century Judaism as a legalistic religion that encouraged the accumulation of merit through works of Law for the purpose of obtaining righteousness in God's sight. Rather, it was centered upon the gracious aspect of God's covenant with Israel. "Works of the Law" were a means of maintaining one's status within God's covenant people, not of assuring personal salvation. While Matera is thus willing to grant that there is a sense in which Galatians is a letter about legalism, he nonetheless insists that "the legalism which Paul opposes is a cultural hegemony rather than a legalistic morality." Since God has sent the Messiah to the covenant people, the "agitators" would have viewed it as reasonable to require Gentile converts to fulfill those works of the Law—circumcision, food laws, Sabbath observance, and so forth—which would assure both their entrance into the covenant people and the maintenance of that covenant relationship.[74]

At this point Matera deals with the question that Francis Watson has left unanswered: "If such is the new interpretation of Galatians, what theological value does this letter have."[75] To answer this question, Matera proposes five theses that are argued in detail in the exegesis of the text:

1. The doctrine of justification by faith needs to be understood anew, not abandoned.

Matera is insistent that Paul's understanding of justification has contemporary social and ecumenical dimensions. Paul argued against a cultural hegemony that attempted the imposition of its customs and practices upon a Gentile minority; today, that minority has become a powerful majority that often seeks to do the same thing. Hispanic Catholics, for example, are often urged, if not compelled, to become Americanized in order to enjoy full membership in the Catholic Church in the United States, but Paul would insist that such cultural assimilation is not a necessary condition of the Gospel. "The faith of Jesus Christ and faith in Christ is essential for full membership in the Church whereas cultural and national differences are a matter of indifference."[76]

2. The social dimension of justification does not eliminate the personal dimension of justification.

It is precisely because something has happened to the individual that the possibility is opened up of a new relationship among communities of people formerly at odds. Because Christ has died for us, we are all equal before God.

3. *Justification* means to be "in Christ."

Paul argues that the Gentiles have a claim to be "seed of Abraham" because they belong to Christ, who is Abraham's singular descendant. Incorporation into Christ through baptism obliterates the distinctions of ethnicity, class, gender—anything that can lead to division. Justification involves being transferred from the realm of the Law to the sphere of Christ, which is marked by life in the Spirit. It is justification precisely as an aspect of being "in Christ" which achieves the fundamental equality of Gentile and Jew that makes cultural differences of no importance.

4. The justified walk according to the Spirit.

There is no contradiction between living a moral, ethical life and justification by faith. Paul expects ethical and moral behavior, refuses to excuse Gentile converts from the moral demands of the Mosaic Law and argues that the Law is fulfilled through the love commandment. The difference between Paul and the agitators is that while the latter invite the Galatians to place themselves in the sphere of the Law, Paul tells his converts to walk by the Spirit.

5. Paul's argument in Galatians is against fellow Jewish Christians.

In Galatians, then, Matera believes, Paul is not arguing against Judaism as such, but against Judaizing tactics of fellow Christians who are Jews; his intended audience is primarily, if not exclusively, Gentile, and he responds to a specific situation. Rather than viewing the letter as a polemic against Judaism, modern Christians would do better to seek the spiritual nourishment that can still be discovered within it.[77]

The Hobgoblin of Inconsistency

Räisänen's criticism of Sanders' position, that it does not account for the way Paul sometimes seems to misrepresent the

Law, may be somewhat overstated, and Räisänen has to a degree
modified his earlier position on Paul's inconsistency, but neither
Sanders nor Räisänen offers a wholly satisfactory explanation of
why Paul should have been so apparently contradictory. Räisänen's earlier position makes Paul inconsistent on a grand scale,
and his more recent suggestion, that Paul's view of the Law
changed in the course of time in the context of polemical situations, does not sufficiently account for the fact that both positive
and negative statements about the Law can appear in the same letter. C. E. B. Cranfield, among many others, criticizes the sweeping
statements Räisänen makes about supposed inconsistencies in
Paul.[78] Stephen Westerholm, after surveying Räisänen's position,
remarks: "At this point, a reader may be inclined to ask how a rea-
sonably intelligent man like Paul could have managed to contra-
dict himself on so many counts within the limits of time imposed
by our common mortality."[79] Similarly, Silva comments, "Some of
the alleged contradictions raise doubts not just about the authority
of apostolic teaching but about Paul's basic intelligence!"[80]

Sanders at least implies that the reason Paul changed his
mind about the Law was due to the overwhelming experience of
his encounter with Christ. However, this still leaves us with the
impression that the personal impact of Christ on Paul was so powerful that he was unable or unwilling to yield on any point that
seemed to threaten the absolute lordship of Christ, even if that led
him to take inconsistent positions. Such a solution seems to leave
Paul open to the charge of extreme subjectivity in his interpretation of the salvific significance of Christ.

The Italian scholar Romano Penna somewhat qualifies the
charge of inconsistency in Paul's view of the Law made by Räisänen, whom he describes as "enthusiastically emphasizing the ten-
sions and contradictions."[81] While stating that "Paul's thought on
the issue is complex and probably never did reach a true logical
maturity," Penna nonetheless suggests that Räisänen's theory of
"secondary rationalization" seems to outstrip his premises.[82]
Though he agrees with Sanders that Paul argues from solution to

plight in emphasizing the superiority of Christ to the Law, Penna restricts the "solution to plight" aspect to Paul's personal experience rather than to the way Paul judges humanity without Christ.[83] Likewise, Penna would further qualify the charge that Paul has deliberately misconstrued the contemporaneous Jewish conception of Law. He asserts that rather than distorting the view of his Jewish contemporaries, Paul censures their view as a reduction of Torah to "Law," a reduction that neglects the typical Jewish combination of Torah as covenant, promise and Gospel.[84] What Paul has done, Penna maintains, is to take up and preserve the ancient Jewish conception of Law with the single difference that henceforth it is transferred to Christ; the result is that universal access to God no longer is mediated by the Law but by Christ.[85] The manner in which Paul has accomplished this is by divorcing the Law from its connection with divine wisdom and then identifying Christ crucified with divine wisdom.[86] This transfer of association with wisdom is similar to Paul's transfer of the meaning of "righteousness" *(dikaiosynē)* earlier identified by Sanders.

Summary

While various aspects of Sanders' position have been called into question, by and large his challenge to the Lutheran interpretation of Paul continues to exercise considerable influence. Nonetheless, he has not managed to convince all scholars that *Paul* did not have a distorted image of the Judaism of his day. R. H. Gundry, in a critique of Sanders[87] (primarily of *Paul, the Law and the Jewish People*), concludes that Paul *did* conceive of Judaism as a religion of works-righteousness, but Gundry's argumentation is somewhat less than convincing. He charges Sanders with too easily explaining away as "hortatory language" the merit terminology in rabbinic Judaism.[88] However, Gundry similarly seems to "explain away" Paul's references to people being judged by their works.[89] More balanced critiques of Sanders are provided by, among others, Morna D. Hooker[90] and John J. Collins.[91]

3
The Law Is Restrictive

A comment by Jean-François Collange in 1973 is reflected to some degree by the authors discussed in this chapter. He suggests that what is wrong with the Law is that it comes to be regarded as a means of salvation and in that way takes the place of God.[1] Thus the fault seems to be not in the Law itself but in what might be termed an incorrect, in this case, idolatrous, perception of the Law. Augustine's opinion was similar in asserting that in Philippians 3:8–9 Paul rejects not the Law but a fleshly attitude. Augustine attributed this attitude ultimately to a lack of proper understanding, and he insisted that Paul was not repudiating either the wisdom of the Jewish Scripture or the prophetic dispensation.[2] In a writing on grace and original sin in the dispute with Pelagius, Augustine refers to those who follow Pelagius as "ignorant of God's righteousness," commenting that they ought to have been able to "recognize" the righteousness from God in the Scriptures.[3]

Questions: J. C. Beker

J. Christiaan Beker agrees with many modern exegetes that the approach of Sanders has been beneficial in preventing pejorative accounts of Judaism as inferior and legalistic, but he also raises some questions:

But the price paid for this irenic treatment is that we are prevented from asking the question that is vital to our understanding of Paul: What actually was the interface between Paul the Pharisee and Paul the Christian? Why did the Christophany evoke such a crisis in his life, one that turned his former allegiance upside down and provoked a view of the Torah that differed considerably from his Jewish-Christian brethren?[4]

Like Sanders, Beker has a concern not to disparage Judaism. According to Beker, Paul sees Christ as both the fulfillment and the end of the Law:[5] "He [Paul] believes that Christ is the surprising answer to Judaism's religious search."[6] Slightly further on, Beker comments: "Paul may misunderstand the Torah, but unlike later Christians he does not treat it in terms of ethnic peculiarities and cultural customs that have no revelational status....Paul may misunderstand Israel's quest for God, but he never interprets Israel in a symbolic sense."[7] Beker views Paul as sincerely believing himself to have remained a Jew even after he became a Christian, but also as misunderstanding Judaism. He differs from the authors to be discussed immediately below, who would not agree that Paul misunderstood either the Torah or Israel's quest for God. In the end, Beker seems to accept that Paul has broken with Judaism. He asks:

Has Paul not really cut the connection between the Exodus-Sinai event and the times of the Messiah in his teaching about the Torah, and so betrayed the inmost heart of Judaism? Above all, to what extent has a "crucified Messiah" and his resurrection qualified the history of the world and inaugurated something radically new...? The Jew asks, "Why hasn't the Messiah come, since the world is so evil?" And the Christian must face the question "If the Messiah has come, why is the world still so evil?" But perhaps the more troublesome question is "How can God love the world that is so evil and obdurate in its hardness of heart that it

crucifies his precious love?"…Around questions like these,
the dialogue must continue.[8]

Identity Markers: J. D. G. Dunn

Beker has put his finger on the question that Sanders, Räisänen, and Francis Watson have not dealt with: What was the interface between Paul the Pharisee and Paul the Christian? Why did
the christophany turn Paul's values upside down? Recent
attempts to answer this question depict Paul, in the light of his
experience of Christ, as changing his perception from one version
of Judaism, which placed high emphasis on ethnic identity markers such as circumcision and dietary restrictions, to another,
which regarded salvation as universally available. Though James
D. G. Dunn is most notably associated with this position, the
emphasis on the restrictiveness of the Law in regard to the availability of salvation was argued earlier (1969) by George Howard,
though with less specific attention to "identity markers."

Howard insists that Paul's remarks about the Law must be
viewed against the background of his missionary activity among
the Gentiles. He interprets Romans 10:4, "Christ is the end of the
Law that *every one* who has faith will be justified," in terms of
Galatians 3:8, which quotes Genesis 12:3, "In you [Abraham]
shall all nations be blessed," contending that Paul understands the
goal of the Law to be the ultimate union of all nations under the
God of Abraham. This blessing for all the nations of Genesis 12:3
is seen as fulfilled in Christ.[9] The problem with the Law is that it
separates Jews from Gentiles and thus tends to prevent the final
unity of all peoples. The death of Jesus ends this "tyranny" of the
Law and allows Gentiles to participate in the blessing of Abraham
equally with Jews.[10]

Like Howard and Francis Watson, Dunn is attentive to the
sociological factors that provide light on Paul's view of the Law,
but unlike Watson, he does not assert such a polarization between
theological and sociological factors, nor has he much tolerance

for the censure of Paul as hopelessly inconsistent in his view of the Law. Dunn has severely criticized both Sanders[11] and Räisä-nen[12] for being willing to accept such a degree of inconsistency in Paul: "…such explanations…are not to be ruled out in principle, of course; but as a way of making sense of the text they must rank as hypotheses of last resort, second only to speculative emenda-tion of the text as disagreeable to good exegesis."[13]

Räisänen has attempted to defend Sanders against the crit-icisms offered by Dunn in a 1985 article in *New Testament Stud-ies.*[14] Räisänen claims an extreme discontinuity between Paul and Judaism but qualifies this by saying that Paul did not initiate the movement toward this break. However, Dunn insists that it is necessary to take into account the complexity of the situations facing Paul before concluding too easily that he was contradic-tory. He asserts that what Paul is contending against in the letter to the Galatians is a wrong attitude toward the Law; such an atti-tude emphasizes the Law's socially defining function of the Jews as a chosen people who possess a collective righteousness that is theirs and no one else's.[15] Dunn maintains that the context of the Letter to the Galatians indicates that by "works of the Law," "Paul intended his readers to think of *particular obser-vances of the Law like circumcision and the food laws,*"[16] those "identity markers" that set off Israel as a nation from those who do not know God.[17]

Thus, the problem is not that there is something wrong with the Law; rather, what Paul criticizes is the wrong attitude toward the Law, an attitude that leads toward exclusivism. The Jewish scholar in rabbinic studies Alan F. Segal approves of Dunn's translation of *erga nomou* (usually translated "works of [the] Law") as "service of the Law" and offers further support for Dunn's argument in earlier works by Ernst Lohmeyer and J. B. Tyson.[18] On the other hand, Joseph Fitzmyer argues against Dunn's interpretation.[19]

Challenges to Dunn: Campbell, Thielman, Penna

D. A. Campbell, however, expresses a caution. In a linguistic and structural study of the terms *pistis* (faith) and *nomos* (Law) in Paul's writings, he contends that the genitive expressions in Paul that combine *pistis* and *Christos* (Christ) are best interpreted by reference to Habakkuk 2:4. Semantically Paul's *pistis* paradigm is more fundamental than his *nomos* paradigm, and the latter may obtain its meaning from its antithetical relation with the former rather than from any content or internal logic of its own. All Paul's prepositions which refer to works and to Law may have little substance of their own, instead referring primarily to a state that is other than one attained by means of *pistis Christou*.[20] Thus, Campbell advises, it is hazardous to base a fully developed theology of Torah on Paul's *nomos* phrases apart from his understanding of *pistis Christou*, regardless of whether such a theology takes the form of "a sociological boundary marker," "covenantal nomism," "legalism" or anything else. "Paul's phrases may contain all these positions at once, and yet probably they designate none of them precisely. The primary meaning of the phrases seems to be to designate any condition which is informed by Law, but which is not in Christ through faithfulness (however this last is conceived)."[21]

In a monograph (1989) on Law in Romans and Galatians,[22] Frank Thielman concurs with Dunn's assessment of the views of Sanders and Räisänen, but nonetheless is of the opinion that Dunn's own discussion, while helpful in understanding some problematic passages, "does not account for all that Paul says about the Law."[23] Thielman further contends that Paul did not, as Sanders holds, argue about the Law from solution to plight, but rather (in Romans and Galatians) from plight to solution, and that in so doing he was in many respects in continuity with at least one stream of contemporaneous Jewish thinking. Schoeps and Beker had somewhat anticipated this view, contending that Paul's argument in Romans 1—5 is a radicalization of the Jewish position on the "evil impulse."[24] Thielman's proposal helps to explain why Paul could have been so open to the revelation of Christ that he experienced:

> ...outside of Christ humanity is subject to the common human plight of disobedience to the Law whereas "in Christ" believers walk by the Spirit and so fulfill the requirements of the Law....[they] have received the eschatological gifts of atonement ([Rom] 3:21–26), forgiveness (4:7), participation in Christ's death (6:1–7:6), and the Spirit (8:1–17). Thus, with the exceptions of the distinctively Jewish requirements of circumcision, dietary regulation, and Sabbath observance, Paul expected his communities to keep the Law in a way that was impossible for those outside.[25]

Penna contends that, despite the title of Thielman's monograph, what the latter really attempts to do is to demonstrate a parallel between the Jewish conception of the eschatological "end" of the Law (God will free Israel both from sin and from the Law's condemnation of sinners) and Paul's view of what has already become of the Law (God has already freed all humanity from both, because the *eschaton* has begun).[26]

While one may not agree with every detail of Thielman's exegesis of the relevant passages, he does seem to have demonstrated that in the Jewish thought of Paul's day there was at least one current that perceived an inability of Israel to obey God's Law and that sought a solution in terms of a future in which God would make it possible for Israel to be free from sin,[27] and there are at least some passages in Paul that appear more comprehensible in this light.

Diversity in Ancient Judaism: John J. Collins

The somewhat earlier (1986) study of Hellenistic diaspora Judaism by John J. Collins is more general in scope but nonetheless relevant to a number of points raised by many of the authors discussed above. It illustrates the presence of a variety of currents in Judaism with different attitudes toward the meaning of covenant, some of which were more exclusive than others.[28] Collins disagrees with the assertion of Sanders that covenantal nomism was the dominant pattern of Judaism from circa 200 B.C.E. to 200 C.E., arguing that the traditional understanding of the covenant, in which the obligations of the Law were regarded as arising from the history of the people, existed side by side with other interpretations, which sought to ground the covenant obligations differently. In apocalyptic, this grounding is seen to come from revelation. In the wisdom literature, it is derived from the observation of human nature that is potentially universal.[29] The variety of patterns Collins has demonstrated makes it possible to view Paul's "reversal of values" as occurring within Judaism rather than in opposition to it. Based on the documents he examines, Collins concludes:

> In virtually all cases the distinctive Jewish requirements such as circumcision and the dietary Laws are ignored. Further, the significance of membership in the actual Jewish community becomes ambiguous. The main requirement for salvation is the right understanding of wisdom, and in nearly all cases this explicitly entails the rejection of idolatry. The Jewish authors may generally have assumed that true wisdom was found primarily within the Jewish community, as Philo surely did. Yet, in principle, the wise and righteous do not necessarily correspond exactly to those who are circumcised....Where the basic understanding was derived from supernatural revelation rather than the traditional formulation of the covenant, the basis for communal identity had been altered and had become more elusive.[30]

Paul as a Christian Jew: Betz, Rowland, Dean, Sloyan, Lambrecht, Wyschogrod, Segal, Boers, Freed, Boyarin

Studies such as those of John J. Collins have led other scholars besides Dunn and Thielman to the conclusion that in becoming

Christian Paul was actually transferring from one Jewish sect to another. This view was articulated as early as 1979 by H. D. Betz, who noted that at the time Paul became a Christian, Jewish Christianity was as yet a movement within Judaism, and Paul's letters indicate that he viewed his call as analogous to that of a prophet like Jeremiah.[31] Christopher Rowland (1985) has accounted for the development of Christianity as a whole as "the most important Messianic sect of Judaism." Within this perspective, he maintains that the event on the Damascus road must be interpreted as the transference of an individual from one Jewish sect to another,[32] parallel to the change that would have occurred if an adherent of the Essenes became a Pharisee.[33]

Rowland asserts that the reason Christ replaced the Law as the key to God's dealings with humanity, in Paul's thought, is located at the heart of the Jewish religious tradition. It was precisely because Paul became convinced that in Christ the messianic age had dawned that his perspective changed. He forsook an interpretation of the Law that was common in noneschatological Jewish groups in favor of one which was dominated by the conviction that the age to come had in fact arrived. "In such a situation," Rowland comments, "it need not surprise us that he should have considered a new attitude appropriate, which still retained the essential obligation typical of the old."[34]

More recently (1990) Alan F. Segal has articulated a similar position, locating Paul, the Jewish Christian, in the line of Jewish apocalyptic mysticism.[35] This tendency to accept Paul as being within the current of Jewish thinking of his day is similarly found in the 1991 dialogue between the Jewish scholar Lester Dean and Gerard Sloyan, professor emeritus of The Catholic University of America,[36] as well as in an earlier (1980) article by the Flemish exegete Jan Lambrecht.[37]

The assertion that Paul continued to regard himself as a Jew continues to be supported by a growing circle of scholars, though occasionally with unusual twists. In 1993, M. Wyschogrod argued that Paul believed that though Gentiles should not adopt circumcision and the Law, that Law continued to be obligatory for Jews who come to faith in Jesus.[38] The previous year Hendrikus Boers had asserted that "works of the law" in Romans 3:28 refers not to good works in general but specifically to what, in Paul's view, restricts salvation to Jews only. However, he also maintained that the perspective of such a radical exclusiveness probably represents the extreme conviction that Paul held before his conversion, not a characteristic Jewish view of his time. Though Paul thought of himself as a Jew, Boers believes, we must distinguish between a historical understanding of first-century Judaism and Paul's own view.[39]

In his 1994 study of Romans and Galatians Boers employs a methodological structure that includes text-linguistics, structuralism, and semiotics to argue that Paul's basic concern in these two letters is the opposition between justification through works of the Law (signifying limitation of salvation to the circumcised) and justification by faith (signifying that salvation was for all). Boers contends that at all levels of Paul's thought there is complete congruity between his negation of justification through works of the Law (Gal; Rom 3:21—4:25) and his positive statements concerning justification through works of the Law in Romans 2.[40] Where Boers differs from other authors who stress the Judaism of Paul is that for the most part they believe that Paul was not totally misunderstanding his Jewish contemporaries, and, as well, that his view of the Law as a Jewish Christian was in accord with views of at least some of his Jewish contemporaries who were not Christian.

The ongoing Jewishness of Paul is a major thesis of E. D. Freed's monograph *The Apostle Paul, Christian Jew: Faithfulness and Law* (1994).[41] Daniel Boyarin, professor of Talmudic Culture at Berkeley, California, has expressed a similar viewpoint, understanding Paul's universalistic views as expressing a radical Jewishness, in his 1994 book *A Radical Jew: Paul and the Politics of Identity.*[42] Some aspects of Boyarin's methodology have been questioned in reviews by N. T. Wright[43] and Terrance Callan.[44] Both feel Boyarin neglects the centrality of Paul's experience of Christ as the major influence in forming his theological and philosophical convictions regarding universalism. Nonetheless, more positively, Dunn acclaims Boyarin as one who "recognizes, as few others have done, what 'the new perspective on Paul' is about," and who for the most part accepts the premise that what Paul was critical of was an ethnocentrism with its accompanying concern to practice "works of the Law," which mark off Jew from Gentile. Further, Dunn notes, Boyarin attempts to remove Paul's response from a legal/moralistic contrast to a particular/universal one. Dunn concludes that this reading of Paul by a Jewish scholar "comes as a breath of fresh air into a room where the smoke of intense internal and introverted Christian debate still hangs heavily."[45] In a 1996 article, Boyarin reiterates his position in a critique of Luther and "neo-Lutherans" such as Westerholm, who are charged with failing to recognize how central the re-creation of universal Israel was for Paul, and also that justification by grace was an essential condition for this.[46]

Summary

According to the scholars in this group, then, Paul was not rejecting the entire Jewish covenant, as Räisänen and Watson have suggested, but a particular interpretation of the covenant and the function of the Law, one which, in Paul's view, overemphasized "identity markers" and had a restrictive perception of the availability of salvation. The attraction Christ would have had for Paul, an attraction strong enough to overturn deeply held convictions, was so strong precisely because it derived from something even more deeply held, the basis of those convictions: the belief in the messianic age, a period of fundamental reversals, initially accompanied by suffering during which the righteous must stand fast, but in which the power of God would emerge triumphant over all other powers.

In most cases, those who have initially attempted to put forth a new perspective on righteousness in Paul have concentrated on

Romans and Galatians but have not dealt in any detail with references to righteousness and Law in Paul's Letter to the Philippians and the Corinthian correspondence. Nonetheless, within the texts they consider and in conjunction with the background material provided by other scholars, they have demonstrated that Paul's thinking about the Law need not be regarded as totally alien to that of contemporaneous Judaism.

4
Luther/Bultmann *redivivus?*

Between Bultmann and Sanders: Byrne, Westerholm, B. L. Martin, Martyn, Hengel and Schwemer

Authors discussed in this chapter have accepted some of the insights of Sanders but nonetheless are unwilling to surrender what they believe to be correct insights associated with the Luther/Bultmann position. An early challenge to Sanders from a Catholic perspective was issued by the Australian scholar Brendan Byrne as an appendix to his 1979 monograph *"Sons of God"—"Seed of Abraham."* Byrne strongly questions whether "works-righteousness" was as totally absent from ancient Judaism as Sanders claims. He concludes that even if Sanders is correct in theory, if works are required to remain "in" the covenant community and if exclusion from that community is equivalent to loss of salvation, then in practice works must be viewed as a means of gaining salvation.[1]

Nonetheless, Byrne is careful to assert that his view of ancient Judaism "does not mean a return to the Bultmann caricature with its excessive stress on *Eigensgerechtigkeit*"[2] (one's "own" righteousness). Byrne places himself in a middle ground between Bultmann and Sanders with a view of Judaism that recognizes the rightful place of the works of the Law within a basically nomistic religion, yet also allows for the operation of divine mercy and ultimately attributes all achievement to God's electing grace. Byrne further maintains that in Paul's total view of God's action in Christ can be found a similar balance between God's demand for obedience and punishment of transgressions; also present is the awareness of a means of atonement, undergirded by God's electing love. This is equivalent to what Sanders perceives as the essential pattern of Judaism as a religion of covenantal nomism. Byrne suggests, however, that Sanders downplays the significance of Paul's apocalyptic perspective. To the extent that Paul differed from the Judaism of his day, Byrne maintains it was a difference of degree: "Paul represents a Judaism *one stage ahead* of Palestinian Judaism in the apocalyptic program. That is, Paul speaks from the perspective of Israel *post adventum Messiae (et huius crucifixi!)*."[3] Thus when Paul is speaking of the righteousness appropriate to the time before the eschaton, his righteousness terminology is precisely that of Judaism; it is when he announces the arrival of the eschaton in Christ that he necessarily refers to the failure of the former righteousness and the availability of righteousness from a new source. While such a proclamation turns the theological expectation of Judaism upside down, it remains couched in a language Judaism understands.[4] In his recent (1996) commentary on Romans, while refraining from specific disagreement with Sanders, Byrne basically argues the same position. The commentary is marked by a great sensitivity to contemporary ecumenical relations between Christians and Jews.[5]

Somewhat later and from a slightly different perspective, while rejecting Räisänen's attempts to explain the inconsistency in Paul's view of the Law, Stephen Westerholm (1988) wholeheartedly endorses the position of Sanders regarding the centrality of Christ.[6] However, he also attempts to demonstrate that Luther's view of Paul was essentially correct,[7] in particular, expressing disagreement with Sanders' interpretation of the meaning of one's "own" righteousness in Romans 10:3, 5–6 and Philippians 3:9.[8] In the final very brief chapter of his book (with reference back to earlier chapters),[9] Westerholm appears to be attempting to answer the charge of inconsistency in Paul, but Westerholm, in turn, has been critiqued by Ziesler.[10] Among other things, one might question the concluding statement of Westerholm in *Israel's Law:* "Nor need the giants of the latter sites [Hippo, Wittenberg and Aldersgate] have perverted the apostle's larger meaning because they show little understanding for the halachic disputes of Paul's day or the perspective of his opponents. Impervious to the problems which preoccupy the moderns, they had eyes for the mountain."[11] Unfortunately, keeping one's eyes on the mountain can result in stumbling over a relatively small obstacle. One might perhaps better argue for more balance between short-and long-range perspectives.

Brice L. Martin, in his monograph on Law in Paul (1989), also appears to accept elements of the positions of both Sanders and Bultmann.[12] Because of Martin's method of treating a number of separate questions related to Paul and the Law (for which his book is a good source of scholarly opinion on various topics), his own position is difficult to determine with exactness. Eugene Hensell, in reviewing the monograph, remarks that Martin "basically nuances several positions generally held by many Pauline scholars, and the influence of E. P. Sanders is evident throughout."[13]

Frank Thielman, another reviewer who has himself contributed substantially to the discussion of Paul and the Law, comments that Martin's work implies that Paul viewed Judaism as a religion of works-righteousness; at the same time, Martin seems to accept Sanders' opinion that first-century Judaism did not regard itself in that manner. This raises the question of whether Paul misrepresented Judaism, as Räisänen maintains, or whether the apostle had insight into the nature of Judaism that was not available to other Jews, as suggested by Bultmann. Thielman reads Martin as apparently agreeing with Bultmann on this question but not dealing with the problem of how Paul expected anyone to believe he had unique insight into the nature of Torah. Martin's proposal that Paul viewed the Law as having both an ostensible and a real purpose is intriguing and raises questions related to God's justice, but these issues are not pursued further within the monograph. The distinction between cultic and moral law likewise invites further discussion that is not forthcoming. In sum, Thielman views Martin as having asked an interesting question and given an answer in the tradition of John Calvin and C. E. B. Cranfield. "The road from the question to Martin's answer, however, is a bumpy ride with little new scenery along the way."[14]

In his recent (1997) Anchor Bible commentary on Galatians, J. Louis Martyn reads the epistle against the background of a thoroughgoing apocalyptic perspective: the cross of Christ totally annihilates all lines of continuity with the past, not simply with Jewish salvation history, but with any human religious construct, including the wisdom of Greco-Roman philosophy. Though in the line of Luther, Barth, and Käsemann in his emphasis on the radical polemic of Paul against the Judaizers, Martyn also exhibits a concern for respectful Jewish-Christian dialogue in his accent on the fact that Paul is not disparaging Judaism as such but rather those preachers who depicted themselves as Christians yet who in reality were undermining the gospel.[15]

Similar in this regard is the view put forth by Martin Hengel and Anna Maria Schwemer in *Paul Between Damascus and Antioch* (1997). Hengel has almost made a career of opposing the interpretations emanating from the German history-of-religions school, which he castigates in no uncertain terms as characterized by a radical prejudice against Judaism. Nonetheless, Hengel and Schwemer describe Luther as one of the greatest interpreters of Paul.[16] One of the main theses argued in this monograph is that Paul's theological insights were essentially fixed at the time of his revelation of Christ and did not undergo development. In particular, this is true of the apostle's view of justification of the godless by grace alone, described as not an insight from the later period of Paul's life, but one that shaped his proclamation from the beginning.[17] Hengel and Schwemer are of the opinion that neither Paul nor any early Christians preached a gospel that can adequately be described as "free from the Law"; rather they were critical of some aspects of Law, and, for Paul in particular, this criticism was christologically and soteriologically motivated.[18] Hengel and Schwemer thus reflect an opinion of Paul's essential consistency that is shared by many of the scholars discussed in this chapter.

Back to Bultmann: Bray, Sandnes, Morris, Kruse

A more unqualified Bultmannian position is set forth in a 1995 article by G. Bray, who challenges the claims made by Dunn and others that the Protestant tradition following Luther has misunderstood the meaning of *dikaiosynē* and related terms and thus misinterpreted Paul's conception of the relation between his inherited Judaism and his faith in Christ. Rather, Bray maintains, it is because of *dikaiosynē,* belonging by right to God but imputed to human beings by faith, that the covenant has come into existence and taken the shape it has.[19] K. O. Sandnes (1996) likewise asserts that neither Dunn nor Watson has succeeded in seriously challenging the Lutheran emphasis on justification by faith as the core of Christian theology, but Sandnes nevertheless admits that this emphasis as concerning mainly the salvation of the individual often represents a narrowing of Paul's perspective.[20]

Likewise, two recent publications by Australian exegetes continue to follow a rather strict Bultmannian position. In a commentary on Galatians aimed at a more general readership, the veteran scholar Leon Morris views the letter as an assault on legalism in the sense of meritorious works.[21] Colin G. Kruse examines all the letters traditionally attributed to Paul, including the pastoral epistles, in an effort to demonstrate a consistency in Paul's view of the Law. He contends that Paul's target was twofold: Jewish particularism and a legalism which held that God's favor could be earned by works of Law.[22]

Righteousness and Personal Relationship with Christ:
Hawthorne, Silva, O'Brien

Authors of three relatively recent major commentaries on Paul's Letter to the Philippians continue to follow Bultmann's interpretation, though with some amplification and qualification. Gerald Hawthorne (1983), sensitive to the immediate context of Philippians 3:9 and the fact that righteousness there is described as coming through faith in Christ, emphasizes strongly the personal and intimate nature of this faith in Christ. Thus the theological emphasis of Bultmann is retained, but Hawthorne likewise recognizes a strongly christological accent in Paul's characterization of righteousness.[23]

Moisés Silva (1988) also calls attention to the christological and personal aspects of righteousness from God. For Silva, the connection between "having righteousness" and "being found in him" (=Christ; Phil 3:9) demonstrates clearly that Paul's doctrine on righteousness is not abstract speculation, but, as Lightfoot had expressed it earlier, the Gospel presented as "a Person and a life." In addition, Silva attempts to go somewhat beyond Bultmann in understanding the meaning of "righteousness from Law." While agreeing with Bultmann that the notion of human effort is part of Paul's characterization, Silva questions why Paul should conceive of righteousness from Law and righteousness from God as mutually exclusive. His solution is that Paul relates righteousness and life so closely (e.g., Rom 1:17, Gal 3:11) that one could almost be defined in terms of another. However, according to Galatians 3:21, the Law cannot give life, and so any righteousness coming from Law is of no value.[24] Silva returns to the connection between righteousness and life in a later work, discussed in the next section of this chapter.

Peter T. O'Brien (1991) maintains that what Paul rejects in Philippians 3:9 is an attitudinal self-righteousness, a moral achievement gained by obeying the Law and intended to establish a claim on God, in favor of a relational righteousness, which is basically a right relationship with God. The relational aspect is also implicitly stressed in O'Brien's understanding of the close tie between the righteousness terminology and the preceding participationist ("in Christ") language of Philippians 3:9a, as well as his recognition that "the knowledge of Christ is not something that is separate from the righteousness of God that comes through faith."[25] Such righteousness has God as its origin, the faith(fulness) of Christ as its basis or ground, and is received by means of faith. Nonetheless, O'Brien does make a qualification: "A zeal for the Law was good; but not the self-righteousness that resulted."[26] While the self-righteous attitude is viewed as a result of the zeal for Law, O'Brien does not seem to insist that it is in all cases a necessary consequence.[27]

O'Brien also differs from a strict Bultmannian position insofar as he refuses to accept the *dikaiosynē ek theou* (righteousness from God) formulation in Philippians 3:9 as a controlling interpretation for the *dikaiosynē theou* (righteousness of God) expressions elsewhere in Paul.[28] Nonetheless, he agrees with Bultmann's stress on the gift character of righteousness with an emphasis that the faithfulness of Christ accents the fact that the righteousness Paul desires is solely a matter of grace.[29] O'Brien has been particularly sensitive to the fact that the participial construction which includes the description of righteousness is syntactically linked with a number of other constructions depicting Paul's relationship with Christ in very personal terms.

The effect of Hawthorne, Silva, and O'Brien's remarks is to somewhat restore a balance in Bultmann's concept of "forensic" righteousness. While Paul could have derived from his biblical background the notion of divine grace placing human beings in right relationship to God, there is also an older biblical notion of this relationship depicted in terms that are more personal. Because it is personal, it makes claims and imposes obligations, but these are not the obligations of an abstract ethical norm. A perceptive discussion of this in relation to Philippians 3:9 was presented some years ago (1970) by Houlden[30] and has recently been restated from a more general perspective by Dunn (1998).[31]

The focus on the connection in Philippians 3:7–11 between righteousness and a personal relationship with Christ to which these authors have drawn attention has not been completely absent in earlier scholars, but neither has it been discussed extensively, despite the fact that commentators routinely remark on the intimate character of the "knowledge of Christ" terminology in Philippians 3:7–11. These scholars thus help to fill out the meaning of Paul's description of righteousness based on faith as it is found in Philippians 3:9. Silva has also raised another issue that scholars from a different perspective have discussed in more detail: the importance of "from Law" as a characterization of the righteousness that is opposed to righteousness from God, thus somewhat deemphasizing the focus on "my" righteousness with its connotation of a prideful attitude.

Paul's Consistent View of the Law:
B. L. Martin, Schreiner, Moo, Silva

Brice L. Martin (1989) sets out to demonstrate that though Paul's view of the Law did undergo some development, this did not result in inconsistency; rather, apparent inconsistency is to be explained by contingent circumstances. Martin contends that while Paul's view of the Law has similarities with Judaism, it differs in that Paul regards the Law as being given that it might be "part of the dilemma of man."[32] The dilemma arises from the moral rather than cultic aspects of the Law.

In several writings, Thomas R. Schreiner argues for consistency in Paul's position on the Law by making some distinctions. He suggests that one must keep in mind that the Mosaic Law has come to an end in its relation to the Mosaic covenant but also that this covenant was always subordinate to the covenant with Abraham, which includes the notion of universal blessing and thus includes the Gentiles.[33] It is because of this that nationalistic Jewish cultic observances such as circumcision and dietary restrictions are no longer binding. However, death to the Law likewise entails liberation from the power of sin that has warped the Law, and this liberation enables believers to obey the moral strictures of the Law under the influence of the Spirit.

Schreiner proposes that there was some distinction in Paul's mind between ritual and moral Law, with reference to 1 Corinthians 7:19, where "commandments of God" probably refer to the moral Law.[34] Nonetheless, Schreiner does not agree that the expression "works of Law" refers to or emphasizes only cultic observances. He asserts that "the failure to be justified by 'works of Law' in Romans 3:20 is due to the Jewish failure to obey the *moral claims of the Law,* not adherence to the ritualistic Law for nationalistic reasons," since in Romans 2:17–29 the Jews are charged with failure to obey the Law even though they *are* circumcised. Schreiner offers three reasons for Paul's denial of the possibility of attaining righteousness by "works of Law": (1) it is impossible for any one to obey the Law perfectly; (2) any attempt to obey the Law to gain righteousness is legalistic and antithetic to the principle of faith; and (3) a salvation-historical shift has taken effect with the death and resurrection of Christ.[35]

It must be kept in mind, however, that regarding the second point Schreiner differs from the strict Bultmannian position that striving to keep the Law would be legalistic and sinful even if it were possible to keep the Law in its entirety. For Schreiner the second reason results from the first.[36] While agreeing with Bultmann and his followers that Paul is opposing legalistic works-righteousness, Schreiner nonetheless is perhaps closer to the position of Wilckens in his contention that "inability to keep the Law must be retained as the foundation stone for Paul's assertion that righteousness cannot be attained by 'works of Law.' This is opposed to Bultmann's view that the very doing of the Law is sinful."[37] Dunn somewhat wryly characterizes Schreiner's position as a " 'have your cake and eat it' thesis."[38]

Douglas J. Moo, in his recent commentary on Romans, advocates a view of the Law based on a broad Pauline corpus that includes the pastorals (1 and 2 Timothy and Titus) as well as Ephesians and Colossians. Moo regards *justification* as a strictly forensic term that points to a legal reality. In Romans 2:14, 3:27, and 7:22–23, "law" does not refer to the Mosaic Torah. In 7:7–25, "I" refers to Paul in solidarity with the Jewish people before or without Christ. In Romans 10:4, *telos* has the connotations of both end and goal. "Works of the Law" refer not primarily to boundary markers, but to the personal legalistic attempt of the Jew. There is no contradiction either within Paul's teaching in Romans or between Romans and the other letters in the Pauline corpus.[39]

In reviewing Moo's commentary, Jan Lambrecht remarks that Moo's defense of Paul's consistency appears stretched at times, but finds a more pervasive problem in Moo's overall outlook. It is not simply that Moo is traditional in rejecting the "new perspective" approach, but that he defends his own theological tradition to an extreme: all human beings are hopeless sinners. Negative expressions such as "doomed to hell,"[40] "predestination to eternal damnation,"[41] and "the final outpouring of his [God's] wrath on the day of judgment"[42] raise questions as to what kind of God is being portrayed and whether this is more Moo's perception than Paul's. If this is *Paul's* belief, Lambrecht asks, is it not in need of critique?[43]

A more balanced view is found in Moisés Silva, who has continued to enter into the discussion of Paul and the Law. Silva reacts to Dunn and the "new perspective" in a 1991 article in which he argues that this perspective results in (1) an underrating of "legalistic" elements that are not only present in early Judaism but endemic to the human condition, and (2) the creation of false dichotomies.[44] Reiterating this point in *Explorations in Exegetical Method* (1996), Silva suggests that rather than insisting that Paul's polemic was either concerned exclusively with the problem of self-righteousness or that it had nothing to do with this but rather with the Jewish concern for national "boundary markers," it might be better to recognize that, in effect, these perspectives are better seen as two sides of the same coin. While Protestant theology had downplayed one side, the new perspective has gone to the other extreme.[45]

For Silva, the doctrine of justification functions as a "conceptual adhesive" and helps in understanding much of Paul's teaching. Nevertheless, he concedes that exegetes who shift attention instead to the Jewish-Gentile question undeniably have a point.[46] The Reformers' exegesis of Galatians 3 requires some qualification, for example, through a greater awareness of Paul's significant concern with being son(s) of Abraham.[47] Silva's concern is to make clear that a full recognition of the redemptive-historical foundation of the message of Galatians does not require abandonment of the traditional Protestant understanding.[48] Nonetheless, his exegetical discussions of various relevant passages in Galatians are concerned less with the notion of an unwarranted self-righteousness than with the relation between righteousness and life, a topic he had addressed in somewhat less detail in his earlier commentary on Philippians.

Unlike many commentators, Silva is observant of the resurrection language in Galatians and its eschatological connection with the theme of life. In commenting on Galatians 2:19–20, he convincingly argues that though such language is not employed in this passage, the notion is both implicit and inescapable. Paul claims that he has died and been raised to new life, and this is an eschatological claim. In addition, Paul has the audacity to formally oppose God and the Law, though this opposition must be nuanced by his remark that it was the Law itself that led to his dying to the Law. This is clear evidence that Paul deliberately speaks of the Law in more than one sense, even if there is a seeming contradiction. Ultimately, the antithesis is between the old existence represented by the Law and new (eschatological) life made possible by the crucifixion of Christ.[49] It is important to note that Silva speaks only of an apparent contradiction. His own conviction is that Paul is a coherent and systematic thinker, though Silva distinguishes between the notion of thinking systematically and writing a systematic treatise.[50]

In his discussion of Galatians 3:2–5, Silva's eschatological awareness again comes to the fore in his remark that, by coupling the *pistis/erga nomou* (faith/works of Law) contrast with the *pneuma/sarx* (flesh/spirit) opposition, Paul has characterized the message of the Judaizers as belonging to an earlier stage of salvation history. He thus effectively argues that a manner of existence founded on works of the Law is obsolete from an eschatological perspective. The question of how one becomes a child of Abraham is taken up in conjunction with Galatians 3:8, 14, and 16. Here Silva remarks that the traditional Protestant exegesis of Galatians 3 did not sufficiently acknowledge the primacy of the Jewish-Gentile issue within this section. He points out an emphasis on promise and fulfillment and, in 3:14, an identification of reception of the Spirit as the fulfillment of the promise to Abraham. Also important is that these verses explicitly refer to the Gentiles; as with 1:16, the evangelization of Gentiles is a characteristically eschatological concept.[51]

In Silva's view, three key texts for understanding the function of the Law in Galatians are 3:21, 3:18, and 3:12. What needs to be stressed in 3:21 is that here Paul specifies in what sense the Law may be viewed positively and in what sense negatively. Positively, it is harmonious with God's saving will expressed in the promise to Abraham. The negative element, represented via a contrary-to-fact conditional sentence, is twofold: (1) the Law cannot impart life; (2) righteousness is not by Law. Paul clearly maintains that the Law is not opposed to the promises by pointing out the conditions under which the Law would have to be regarded as conflicting with the promises: If the Law were a source of righteousness, that is, if it could impart life, then it would compete with the promises. However, in reality the Law cannot impart life. It did not thwart the promise but aided the promise by imprisoning all humanity under sin (3:22–23).

The linking of "law" *(nomos),* "could" *(dynamenos,* "being able") and "life" *(zōopoiēsai,* "to make alive") recalls Romans 8:3, where, in addition to lexical similarity, substantive agreement in content is present. Romans 8:3 contrasts two principles, the Mosaic Law, associated with sin, as in Galatians 3:22–23, and the Spirit that gives life, corresponding to the saving promise of God in Galatians 3:14. Further, the verse from Romans makes clear what is only implicit in the text from Galatians, namely, that the obstacle that renders the Law impotent for salvation is the weakness of the flesh. Human beings are dead in their sins and trespasses, and as a result the commandments are of no avail. Without spiritual life, humanity cannot accomplish what is written in the Law and thus comes under a curse.

A substantial, if not formal, parallel to the conditional clause of Galatians 3:18–21 appears in 3:18, which uses the term *inheritance* as equivalent to the "righteousness" and "life" of 3:21 (cf. 3:29). Though Paul employs what is grammatically termed a "real" condition, this does not mean that he accepts the reality of the condition; the point is that the inheritance cannot depend on the Law, or the promise would be invalidated (Gal 3:17). The fact that 3:21 is essentially a more specific restatement of the argument of 3:18 has implications for exegesis.

Commonly in the Lutheran tradition and among Dispensationalist interpreters, but sometimes among Reformed theologians as well, the third chapter of Galatians has been cited as evidence that Paul saw the Law and the promise as opposed. On the contrary, Silva maintains, it can be argued that the burden of the passage is precisely to deny any such opposition. The polemic vein of the passage strongly suggests that Paul is reacting to accusations from the Judaizing opponents. There is no reason to believe that these opponents desired the nullification or even alteration of the Abrahamic covenant; every indication was that they wished that Gentiles should participate in the inheritance of the children of Abraham, but they seem to have argued that this blessing could only be received by submitting to circumcision and thus becoming Jews.

What raised the question regarding the compatibility of the two covenants was most likely Paul's insistence that circumcision was unnecessary since the inheritance rested on God's promise to Abraham. The Judaizers may have argued that Paul was thus pitting the two covenants against each other. Paul's defense is that it is the Judaizers who, in effect, oppose Law and promise because, by not recognizing the gracious character of the promise to Abraham, they have elevated law keeping to a level it was never intended to occupy; thus, even if unintentionally, they set aside the promise. All this is implied in Galatians 3:17, and thus 3:18, introduced by the conjunction *gar* (for), functions logically to demonstrate the implied charge of 3:17. Having assumed throughout his argument that the premise of the Judaizers is that the inheritance comes from the Law, Paul identifies this basic point of dispute, a point which he adamantly refuses to concede because it is in opposition to the scriptural principle earlier supported by Habakkuk 2:4. The antithesis is not between Law and promise as such but between inheritance by Law and inheritance by promise. Paul does not castigate the Law in general, but only the notion that the Law is a source of life.

Paul's repudiation in Galatians 3:21 of the idea that the Law produces life can be helpful in understanding his use of two citations from Scripture, Leviticus 18:5 and Habakkuk 2:4, in Galatians 3:12. The passage from Leviticus appears to be flatly contradicted by Galatians 3:21. However, the restriction of the criticism of "Law" in 3:21 to "Law as source of Life," together with the immediately preceding context of 3:11, where Paul focuses specifically on one aspect of the Law—its justifying function—indicates that in 3:12 Paul is not speaking of Law in its entirety. Indeed, Silva believes, Paul most likely *did* view the Law as *leading to* life, but energetically denied that it could be the *source* of righteousness and life. Thus, placing himself squarely in the Reformed tradition, in opposition to both orthodox Lutheranism and classic Dispensationalism, Silva vigorously maintains that Paul's critique of the Law has reference only to its soteriological function; only in this respect was the Law preparatory and not life-giving.[52]

Even if the eschatological overtones earlier in the letter might have been overlooked in a cursory reading of the text, Silva insists, Galatians 3:19—4:7 leaves no room for doubt that the time of Law as a redemptive-historical period has ended. This "end" of the Law is connected with the coming of faith, and the new stage in salvation history is equated with the fullness of time, the time when God's promises are fulfilled beyond expectation. Gentiles are now considered not merely children of Abraham (3:29) but children of God (3:26, 4:6–7).

Silva believes, however, that three points deserve further consideration: (1) Paul's emphasis on the universal "objective" events of salvation history does not exclude a concern for the personal "subjective" application of those events (3:27, 4:5, 4:6). (2) Paul easily moves back and forth between the Jewish and Gentile experience, for example, when he links the Galatians' former ceremonialism in the pagan milieu with the legal requirements of Judaism (4:8–11). The experience and sense of spiritual confinement that Paul depicts was by no means the exclusive property of Israelites who lived under the Law. (3) The fact that the time of the Law has reached its conclusion does not mean that the Law no longer exists or functions experientially. Conversely, to own that the period of faith begins with the advent of Christ does not mean that faith was not experienced before the cross. Nonetheless, the two perspectives must be kept distinct.[53]

In commenting on Galatians 4:25–27, Silva refers to a 1993 article of Karen H. Jobes,[54] who suggests that Paul's citation from LXX Isaiah 54:1 advances Paul's argument because, in reality, Sarah *has* given birth. The key is the resurrection of

Jesus, which Paul has construed as the miraculous birth that would transform Jerusalem the barren one into the faithful mother-city Jerusalem according to Isaiah 26:1. Acceptance of Jobes's reading, in Silva's view, would demonstrate that the resurrection of Jesus informs the argument of Galatians at its most basic level.[55]

In his discussion of passages from chapters 5 and 6 of Galatians, Silva points out the parallelism between 5:6 and 6:15 (and also their connection with 1 Corinthians 7:19), where the notion of "faith working through love" is unambiguously identified with the new creation, manifested in behavior that includes fulfillment of the Law of Christ by bearing one another's burdens. However, the strongly ethical character of 5:16–26 should not lead one to neglect the eschatological dimension evident in 5:24–25, which echoes 2:20. The basic continuity between realized and future aspects of the *sarx/pneuma* (flesh/spirit) contrast is apparent in 6:8, a verse that explicitly states what is implicit in the letter as a whole.[56]

The closing verses, Galatians 6:13–17, emphasize the apocalyptic antinomy that informs Paul's argument.[57] Though the themes of righteousness and faith are not explicit here, these verses demonstrate that central to Paul's argument is the assertion that the cross of Christ is the decisive event in redemption history, an event that brings the old era to an end and inaugurates the new creation.[58] The closing thus sharpens the fundamental theological issue of the letter. The mortal weakness of the "other gospel" is its incompatibility with the cross of Christ. If this is granted, then Paul's basic critique, Silva concludes, was that his opponents failed to perceive the eschatological meaning of Christ's crucifixion and thus sought to remain in the old "world" of circumcision; on the contrary, those who belong to the new creation share in that crucifixion and thus no longer live to the old age, but according to another pattern of existence, Spirit-led, and thus comprise the true, eschatological Israel of God.[59]

Summary

The major differences between the scholars discussed in this chapter, particularly this final section, and those treated in chapter 5 are that the latter are far less interested in defending a strong Luther/Bultmann position (though they may not disagree that some elements of it should be retained) and are more concerned with the question of Paul's overall consistency.

5
Expanded Horizons

The primary question of authors discussed in this chapter is "How can Paul's view of the Law be demonstrated to be coherent and consistent?" Regarding this issue, the scholars in this group generally agree with those treated in chapter 3. However, they attempt to move the discussion to a wider arena by expanding the discussion beyond Galatians and Romans to include other letters of Paul. Specifically, they make reference to the Thessalonian and Corinthian correspondence, as well as the letter to the Philippians as a whole, not simply Philippians 3:9. While Philippians 3:9 has often been referred to since Bultmann, it had not until recently been discussed in great detail, nor had the remainder of Paul's letter to the Philippians entered into the discussion. Some discussion of the Corinthian correspondence had been present in authors such as Ernst Käsemann, who attempted to modify Bultmann's description of the character of righteousness from God, but authors who initially advocated and developed the "new perspective" on Paul focused mainly on Galatians and Romans. For many of the exegetes considered in this chapter, what is wrong with the Law, in Paul's view, is its connection with sinfulness.

Jan Lambrecht and His Students

In a 1986 article, Jan Lambrecht demonstrates in a close study of Galatians 3:10–14 that on the basis of this passage one cannot accuse Paul of the charge of inconsistency in his view of the Law. He notes that some support from this passage could be claimed by scholars from four different perspectives: (1) that of Wilckens, with his insistence on the association of the Law with sin and on the fact that the Law cannot be kept in its entirety; (2) the Bultmannian position, which views the Law as inherently associated with prideful self-righteousness even if it could be kept in all respects; (3) the position of Dunn, that by "works of Law" Paul is primarily referring to "identity markers" such as circumcision, food laws, and calendar observances; and (4) that of Sanders, that the Law does not lead to righteousness because righteousness is found only through Christ.

Lambrecht definitively rejects the Bultmannian position, arguing that the reason a curse is incurred by those who strive for righteousness by doing works of Law is due to their sinful inability to keep the Law in its entirety. Observance of cultic practices such as circumcision is wrong not because it is "self-righteous" in the sense of being prideful, but because since the coming of Christ such striving for one's "own" righteousness misunderstands God's initiative in Christ. Lambrecht concludes by cautioning that this is only one of many Pauline texts on the subject and that other passages must be considered in order to fill out the picture. In particular, Romans 10:2–3 and Philippians 3:3–11 should be examined to ascertain whether they suggest that Paul is rejecting an attitude of prideful works-righteousness.[1]

An American student of Lambrecht, John Buckel, in his 1993 monograph on Galatians, agrees with Sanders that "Paul's major difficulty with the Torah as a viable means to justification is that the Law is not Christ"[2] and that a major problem for Paul is that the Law does not make salvation universally available.[3] Buckel likewise finds it difficult to accept the sociological thesis of Francis Watson, despite agreement with the latter that analysis of biblical texts should take account of the social and historical content of those texts. Buckel contends that only a few verses even remotely suggest that the reason Paul rejected the Law as a means of obtaining righteousness was to make it easier for him to attract more converts to Christianity. Further, Buckel remarks, even those passages that Watson employs to argue his position are not persuasive. For example, nothing in 1 Corinthians 9:21 invalidates the view that "Paul's understanding of the Law is based on his experience of the risen Lord and/or on theological reflection." Moreover, Paul's advice concerning food offered to idols in 1 Corinthians 8 *is* based on such reflection.[4]

Lambrecht and his student Richard W. Thompson, in a joint study of the implications of Romans 3:27–31 (1989),[5] are similar to many of the scholars discussed in the previous two chapters in denying the charge of inconsistency in regard to Paul's view of the Law. They also would agree that Paul stresses the universal availability of salvation in Christ, but they tend more to emphasize that this universality includes *Jews* as well as Gentiles. Though their discussion is limited to a close study of Romans 3:27–31 linked with Romans 8:4 and Romans 4, the consistency in Paul's view that they attempt to demonstrate within the letter to the Romans is somewhat distinctive. They disagree with scholars who would assert that when Paul, in Romans 3:31, claims that he upholds the Law, what he really means is that he upholds only part of it, the moral Law—the part that has to do with ritual or ceremonial Law is excluded.

On the contrary, Lambrecht and Thompson suggest that "when Paul claims to uphold the Law, he means the Mosaic Law in its entirety."[6] They question, first, whether our contemporary viewpoint, which regards ceremonial and cultic Laws as in some sense secondary or marginal to the moral aspects of the Law, really applies to Paul, who as a first-century Jew would have considered the entire Law as given by God and each of its requirements as rooted in the will of God. Secondly, they maintain, Paul "no doubt" viewed the individual commands of the Law as collectively expressing the will of God, as is partially evident in Romans 2:21–22. There, in his charge of disobedience to the Law, Paul includes moral elements such as stealing and adultery and cultic elements such as idolatry. Again, in Romans 2:25–29, he speaks of circumcision, a ritual element, and its relationship to obedience to the Law in its entirety.

Nonetheless, Lambrecht and Thompson do not hold that, for example, the command to circumcise is of the same weight as prohibitions against murder or adultery, and they do grant that Paul subordinates circumcision to a position within the moral life.[7] They also recognize that Paul went beyond repeating the traditional Jewish understanding of how the Law was to be upheld. Paul *does* reinterpret both the significance and the meaning of diverse aspects of Law, notably circumcision, but the very act of reinterpreting the Law is an exercise in upholding it. In particular, Lambrecht and Thompson connect the positive value of circumcision in Romans 4, as well as its relation to faith, with the reference to upholding the Law in 3:31: "The discussion at Romans 4:9–12 demonstrates that it is precisely through faith and the righteousness that comes by faith that circumcision receives its true meaning and value, as a sign of that righteousness....Paul's teaching on righteousness by faith, far from destroying the significance of circumcision, actually upholds it for Abraham and Jewish Christians."[8]

In a 1991 article Lambrecht returns to Galatians 3:10–14, reiterating his earlier treatment of this passage with some modification, in particular expressing some hesitation about limiting the interpretation of "works of the Law" according to Dunn's suggestion, but coming to essentially the same conclusions as in his earlier study of the passage. The reason works of the Law do not justify is that "all people, Jews and Gentiles alike, have sinned and are thereby guilty. In order to redeem them from this sinful and cursed situation Christ must become a substitutionary curse. Jews can do works of the Law; these are not wrong in themselves.

But because of other works not done, they do not justify."[9] However, in a final section Lambrecht attempts to broaden the horizon, taking into account the problem of other negative utterances about the Law.

Lambrecht initiates this "Hermeneutical Reflections" section with three considerations: (1) Contrary to Dunn's suggestion, probably in Galatians and most certainly in Romans, the expression "work(s) of the Law" designates the entire extent of works required by the Law. (2) Romans 9:30—10:4 and Philippians 3:4–9, which respectively include references to Israel's "own" righteousness and "my [= Paul's] own" righteousness, must be examined to determine whether they focus on works–righteousness. In the text from Romans, Lambrecht finds the contrast to be between the impotent Jewish way of salvation, that of the Law, and God's new initiative in Christ, the way of salvation through faith. The passage from Philippians illustrates Paul's faithful if extremist obedience to Law as a particular case of typical Jewish righteousness based on Law that is opposed to righteousness based on faith. Paul claims in Philippians 3:2–3 that it is "we" (= Christians) who are the circumcision. Since the advent of Christ, even zealous obedience to the Law is hopeless and does not lead to salvation, and if it is coupled with rejection of Christ, it is also tragically sinful. (3) Romans 4:2–6 and 9:10–13 also require interpretation. Lambrecht notes that the first passage speaks of "works" in a more general sense than "works of the Law." All human striving is preceded by the justifying grace of God, which is a free gift. Romans 9:10–13 likewise describes the election of Jacob as a gift of grace. Again, not only works of the Law but all human works are eliminated.

Lambrecht next addresses the question of whether "without the works of the Law" means that the Christian is no longer obliged to obey the commands of the Law. Here he refers to a 1989 study of Schreiner[10] which suggests that nationalistic cultic observances have been abolished because the Mosaic Law in relation to the Mosaic covenant is no longer in effect and that believers are liberated from the power of sin, which perverts the Law. Paul's parenetical material demonstrates that the moral Law continues in force though ritual prescriptions are no longer valid. Lambrecht cautions, however, that Paul neither presents his parenesis as a new Torah nor does he support his exhortations by scriptural argument, despite the fact that he uses Scripture abundantly in presenting his own vision of Law. In addition, Paul does not say that Christians "do" the works of the Law, but rather that they "fulfill" the Law. "Doing" what the Law prescribes is no longer focused upon; it is Christ or the Spirit of Christ who is the source of Christian life and conduct.

A final consideration is the relevance this discussion has for contemporary Christian living. Lambrecht offers three suggestions: (1) While legalism existed in Paul's day and our own and Paul would not have sanctioned it, his primary focus is equal treatment of Jews and Gentiles; for all without distinction the way to salvation is that of faith in Jesus Christ. (2) The great lesson of Galatians 3:10–14 and of Paul's vision of the Law as a whole is the priority of God's grace; being blessed by this grace, apart from human merit, is "the overwhelming salvific mystery."(3) The distinction Sanders makes between "getting in" and "staying in" risks limiting the priority of God's grace to the initial justification and losing sight of the fact that Christians need God's grace always and everywhere. Nonetheless, Paul's clear emphasis on the gift quality of grace "would be misunderstood if we are not simultaneously convinced that after justification a Christian, through Christ's mighty Spirit, must act in love and in this way fulfill the Law."[11]

Brendan Byrne has recently (1996), apparently independently, and with some differing emphases, expressed views to some degree similar to those of Lambrecht and Thompson. He maintains that the universal prevalence of sin, which included the covenant people within its range, necessitated the abandonment of any quest for eschatological righteousness under the Law.[12] While Paul obviously believed that the central ethical values of the Law, as distinct from its ritual prescriptions, remained in force for the believer, the apostle nonetheless does not explicitly make a distinction within the content of the Law, nor does such a distinction appear to have been made in Judaism. However, Paul does, at least implicitly, appear to distinguish between what the Law prescribes *as law* and the values that it enshrines as expressing God's will for humanity in an ethical sense. For believers, Byrne suggests, these values are not imposed as law, from without, but are fulfilled from within through the gift of the Spirit. Paul's statement that love is the fulfillment of the Law (Rom 13:10) is metaphorical only, a means of communicating to doubtful converts that love is a more than sufficient way to carry out everything that was required by the Law in the old dispensation.[13]

As a student of Lambrecht who has worked extensively on Paul's letter to the Philippians, I have examined Philippians 3:7–11 in some detail in an attempt to ascertain the characteristics of the two kinds of righteousness referred to in this passage.[14] A close study of the grammar and syntax of the passage[15] had convinced me that the "righteousness from God" of Philippians 3:9 is semantically and syntactically related to a number of expressions within the passage that describe Paul's eschatological goal from different perspectives. All but one of these express the goal in terms of the perfection of an already existing situation or experience. "My own righteousness," on the other hand, is a relatively unique expression, as well as being perhaps the most problematic phrase within the participial construction of v. 9. Its meaning, therefore, should be ascertained from its context.

Many authors have suggested a chiastic structure in Philippians 3:9 as providing a clue to the nature of "my own righteousness," but the proposals disagree in details and almost invariably leave out some elements of the comparison. In syntactic terms, there is no chiasm, but rather an opposition between "my own righteousness" and "that which is through faith in Christ." Each of these phrases is further qualified, the first by "that which is from Law," the second by "the righteousness from God based upon faith." "Faith" occurs in both descriptions of the type of righteousness Paul seeks. Though the wider context of Philippians 3:2–21 includes a dispute with opponents who advocated circumcision, Philippians 3:7–11 is dominated by the sense of the all-surpassingness of the knowledge of Christ, which has given Paul a new perspective. What Paul does in v. 9 then is to describe his former perception of righteousness and the new perception gained from the perspective of his knowledge of Christ; this enables him to now recognize that the past sufferings of Christ and present sufferings of Christians are the birth pangs of the messianic age. Thus, the reference to the righteousness that is through faith occurs in a context in which the christological perspective has primacy.[16]

In addition, the righteousness Paul seeks has a participatory character, since the context links it with expressions describing participation in Christ. A survey of other texts in Paul indicates that in the letters of Paul righteousness is linked normally, rather than exceptionally, with participationist language, a further indication of the primacy of the christological perspective in Paul's concept of righteousness. The faith on which righteousness rests is characterized by relying on, or having confidence in, God's promise as fulfilled in Christ, even to the point of "glorying" or "boasting" in Christ (Phil 3:3). To rely on flesh or on the Law is to have a false perception since such action ascribes a power to flesh or the Law that they do not possess. In addition, such reliance does not take into account that something that is good or neutral, but is not God, can be co-opted by the sphere of sin. For a good Jew, to treat anything that is not God as God is idolatry, and Paul's realization that this was what he had unwittingly fallen into may account for the strong language with which he describes his former "gains" in Philippians 3:7–8. In Philippians Paul makes clear that if faith means relying on Christ for final salvation, it implies that trust in God, in Christ, will provide the necessary strength to adhere to that goal in present circumstances as well.[17]

There are grounds in Philippians 3:7–11 to support the view that Paul's encounter with the risen Christ effected a conversion from one form of Judaism to another. The discussion in 3:1–6 is the kind of dispute that only makes sense in a context in which both parties consider themselves and their antagonist(s) as Jews or claiming to be such. Bultmann's interpretation is excluded because Paul is not only rejecting Jewish privileges in Philippians 3:7–11, but any kind of privilege; *every* gain, whether of birth or Paul's own striving, is now perceived as loss. Paul either does not (as Bultmann does) presume that the meaning of "my own righteousness" is self-evident, or he realizes that it could be misinterpreted without qualification. He therefore qualifies it by the attributive construction "that which is from Law." Syntactically, the second expression defines the first, not vice versa. The aspect of singularity rejected is not that of individual singularity, but of exclusiveness that results from regarding salvation as restricted to those who consciously obey the Law. As in Romans 10:3, the root error is ignorance, not arrogance. Paul recognizes his error from the perspective of his knowledge of Christ Jesus as Lord. Far from criticizing his own desire to be blameless as characteristic of arrogance, he prays that the Philippians will be "pure and blameless in the day of Christ" (1:10) and "without blemish" (2:15).[18]

Rather than rejecting the biblical concept of knowledge of God, Paul's assertion in Philippians 3:7–11 amounts to a bold identification of knowledge of God with knowledge of Christ. Except for Abraham, to whom, according to Galatians 3:8, the Gospel was preached beforehand, Paul never refers to any Jew who is not a Christian as a "believer." The faith on which righteousness rests cannot separate faith in God from faith in Christ. Räisänen thus concludes that Paul is simply replacing the exclusive claims of Judaism with exclusive christological claims, but the underlying assumption present in Philippians 3:7–11 and throughout Paul's writings is that the relationship Paul describes between himself and Christ is available to anyone willing to accept it in faith. The relationship may be a privilege, but access to the relationship is not restricted by privilege, and within the relationship, conventional designations of privilege or superiority do not apply (Gal 3:28). While the righteousness that Paul seeks is clearly a gift of God, the gift demands a response that includes human effort. In Philippians 2:12 the community is enjoined to "work out *your own* salvation with fear and trembling; for God is at work in you"[19] (*RSV*, emphasis mine).

Perhaps the basic question in understanding Philippians 3:9 is not "What is wrong with the Law?" but "What is wrong with Paul's former perception of the Law?" The contrast is not between prideful human effort and God's grace, but between two human attitudes, two kinds of perception, one of which is characterized by ignorance that in Christ the messianic age has dawned and another that consists in "the knowledge of Christ Jesus my Lord." The power in this passage is not described in terms of a new creation, as Käsemann suggests. It is described as a power which in Paul's past has precipitated a reversal of perception, in the present conforms him to the death of Christ, and in the future (Phil 3:20–21) will transform him and his sister and brother Christians into the likeness of the glorious Christ.[20]

The study of John J. Collins referred to previously has pointed out an identification of the wise with the righteous which suggested to me that further exploration of the connection between Paul's notion of righteousness and his biblical Wisdom background might be relevant to the discussion of Paul and the Law. I have explored this in the final chapter of my 1996 monograph on Philippians 3:7–11,[21] pointing out connections among knowledge *(gnosis),* wisdom *(sophia),* and righteousness *(dikaiousynē)* terminology in biblical Wisdom literature. Examples include Proverbs 1:20–22, and chapters 2—5 and 16—19 of the Book of Wisdom, which deal with the death and vindication of the righteous one.[22] Further, I have explored the Wisdom ambience of the undisputed letters of Paul, in which links with righteousness and *sophia/gnosis* terminology consistently appear, and not always in a polemical context.[23] I thus belong firmly in the camp of those scholars who view Paul as being predominantly influenced by his Jewish heritage and continuing to regard himself as a Jew. I believe it is precisely the perspective of divine Wisdom so apparent in the biblical Wisdom literature, and indeed in Paul's entire biblical heritage, which made it possible for him to undergo the astounding reversal of values which led him to enthrone Christ in the place formerly occupied by the Law within Judaism, just as the authors of Sirach (Ecclesiasticus) 24:1–29 and Baruch 3:9—4:4 had earlier identified Woman Wisdom with Torah.

Law under the Power of Sin:
Klyne Snodgrass and Robert Sloan

In 1988, Klyne Snodgrass suggested that it would be helpful in the discussion of Paul's apparently inconsistent statements about the Law to recognize that, for Paul, the determinant for the Law is the sphere in which it is located. While its rightful use is in the sphere of Christ, it can be "taken over" and used by sin. Within the sphere of sin, the Law is negative and causes death, but in its proper sphere it expresses God's will and is for life (Rom 8:7, 7:10). The notion of spheres of influence, also operative in Galatians, clarifies Paul's use of *nomos* in Romans 3:27–31, 4:13–16, 5:20, 7:1–6, and 7:21—8:7.[24]

The basic idea represented here has been recognized more or less independently by a number of authors, some of whom use "power" *(dynamis)* or "sphere" language, as, for example, Clinton E. Arnold, in his 1992 monograph *Powers of Darkness,* who points out that Paul depicts both the Jewish Law and pagan religion as having been exploited by "Satan and his powers."[25] Others employ terminology that is more colloquial. Fitzmyer, for example, speaks of the Law as a "henchman" of sin (translating the Greek *dynamis* as "force"),[26] while David Wenham[27] and Byrne both describe the Law as having been "hijacked" by sin. Somewhat colorfully, Byrne portrays the Law as "the helpless tool of the machinations of the real culprit, sin."[28] Earlier,

Heinrich Schlier (1977)[29] and Ulrich Wilckens (1978–82),[30] in their respective commentaries on Romans, had understood the "law of sin" in Romans 7:22–26 as referring to the Mosaic Law as dominated and corrupted by the power of sin, and they are followed in this interpretation by John Paul Heil (1987).[31] The fundamental notion of "powers" or "spheres of influence" appears to be almost self-evident for a number of scholars, but Snodgrass seems to be unique in having proposed it as a means of reconciling apparent inconsistencies in Paul's view of the Law; Robert B. Sloan further expands and develops this notion.

A 1991 article on Paul and the Law by Sloan[32] explains the attraction of Christ for Paul in terms of his messianic expectations, incorporating the notion of spheres of power suggested by Snodgrass.[33] Sloan regards the Law as having come under the power of sin. Like Rowland and Segal, Sloan regards Paul as one who remained within Judaism. While agreeing with Dunn's contention that Sanders and Räisänen leave Paul open to a charge of inconsistency that is unsatisfactory,[34] Sloan nonetheless is of the opinion that Dunn's solution—that Paul's criticism of "works of the Law" is not a criticism of the Law in itself but only a repudiation of the use of the Law as an exclusionary and racially narrow means of social identity—is likewise inadequate because such a view shifts the blame from the Law itself to its abuse, distortion, or misunderstanding. In so doing, Sloan maintains, it too much softens references to the Law as "something which 'enslaves' (Rom 6:15; 7:1–4), 'produces death'/'kills' (Rom 7:5,8–13; II Cor 3:6), 'works wrath' (Rom 4:15), 'increases sin' (Rom 5:20; 7:5, 8–13; cf. Gal 3:19), and from which one in Christ finds 'liberation' (Rom 6:15, 7:6; Gal 3:23, 25, 4:4, 5; 5:1; II Cor 3:14–17)."[35]

Sloan sets forth five assertions on which he bases his further argumentation: (1) The unity of Torah must be maintained; Paul may use dualistic language to explain the dual work (both saving and sinister) of the Law, but he is not in fact speaking of two Laws. In particular, the dualistic language of Romans 7:7–25 reflects the human situation under the two conflicting functions/works of the one Law. In his insistence on the unity of Torah, Sloan's position is in agreement with that of Lambrecht and Thompson. (2) Both Paul and first-century Judaism affirm that the Law is given by God and thus is holy, righteous, and good. Paul may sometimes appear to have stretched the connection between God and Law rather thin, but in Paul's mind this connection is never completely broken. (3) The Law points to Christ. (4) The Law is both revealer of the divine will and agent of sin. (5) The sinister function of the God-given Law that has been co-opted by sin explains passages such as Romans 5:20, 6:14, and 7:1–7.[36]

The presumable inconsistency in Paul's view of the Law can be explained if it is accepted that Paul regards the good Law of God as subject to usurpation by the powers of sin. In the act of revealing the divine will, the Law is drawn into the power sphere of sin, and sin thus acquires an energy (1 Cor 15:56) that is stronger than the energy of the human will, which in this situation can recognize the validity of the Law of God but not adapt its behavior accordingly.[37] A number of biblical texts[38] associate God with spirits of both good and evil function. "If the ability to attribute works of evil/judgment to the Lord was already available to Paul in his religious/scriptural tradition, why is it considered unthinkable that Paul could have maintained both the goodness of the law as something given by God *and* the liability of the law as an instrument of the powers of sin?"[39]

Here, like Snodgrass, Sloan understands Paul to be thinking in terms of "power spheres" (cf. Rom 8:2–8, Gal 5:16–17). The good Law of God comes under the sphere of the flesh, of sin and death. The only force strong enough to oppose this evil sphere is the sphere of the Spirit, that is, being "in Christ," and the only way of transferring to this sphere is by hearing and believing the Gospel. The Law thus can be removed from the sphere of sin and can operate in the sphere of the Spirit. Regarded in this light, Paul's positive allusions to the Law and his demands for Christian obedience are not contradictory.

Sloan suggests that while Paul developed this attitude to the Law within the framework of Judaism and applied it to Israel as a whole, this view of the Law arose from Paul's own personal experience. Lambrecht had earlier (1974–75) made the same point with regard to Romans 7 in "Man Before and Without Christ: Rom 7 and Pauline Anthropology"[40] and returns to the theme in more detail in a 1992 monograph, *The Wretched "I" and Its Liberation: Paul in Romans 7 and 8.*[41] In a 1983 study, *Psychological Aspects of Pauline Theology,* Gerd Theissen similarly concludes that what Paul concealed in Philippians 3—his view of his pre-Christian period in the light of the knowledge of Christ—is what he develops in Romans 7: "...the shadow side of his zeal for the Law. Romans 7 is the result of a long retrospective bringing to consciousness of a conflict that had once been unconscious. Paul considers this conflict to be universally human."[42] Sloan describes Paul's attitude as existential, though not based on prior psychological frustration.[43] Rather, in the light of the Damascus christophany,

> Paul came to view [his former existence] in retrospect as psychologically destructive, diabolically motivated, and theologically/eschatologically blinkered. That is, his zeal for the law had blinded him to the very hope toward which his zeal and religious devotion in principle and intention drove....Paul's zealous blindness was not for him explicable in the usual kinds of psychological blindness which we like to posit as a feature of ideological zeal. Rather, Paul came to believe that his devotion to the law had opened him up to the powers of evil. As one zealously under the law, he had (unwittingly) become a victim of the powers of sin. It was therefore the law as given through angels, and thus itself under the powers, that explained for Paul the vulnerability of one under the law to the powers of sin and darkness (and explains for us the vehemence of Paul's warnings to any and all who would return to that sphere).[44]

Sloan thus argues that Paul could only explain the blindness of both himself and Israel to the Messiah as a function of their zeal, that is, their devotion to the Law, but a Law that had come under the power of sin. Nonetheless, in God's mysterious purposes, Paul was able to believe that even the sinister work of the Law was part of the redemptive process, since this sinister function is exercised within the framework of God's saving history. Israel's devotion to the Law has provoked the assault of the powers of sin in such a way that, if anything, there is an explicit lessening of responsibility for the failure to do good (Rom 7:17). While Paul does not relieve either Israel or himself of moral responsibility, such responsibility must be understood not only in terms of obstinacy and failure, but also of laudable dedication to the Law and pursuit of righteousness. In Romans 9—11 and 7:14–25, "it is the experience of a commendable devotion that came to a tragic end which, in the mercy of God, also became his instrument of salvation to Jew and Gentile alike, to all who call upon the name of the risen Lord."[45]

Contextualizing the Discussion: Frank Thielman

Frank Thielman, in his 1994 monograph *Paul and the Law: A Contextual Approach,* closely examines Paul's view of the Law in the contexts of Judaism, the circumstances of the letters, and the language and argumentation of each letter. He concludes that Paul's position on the Law was a complex evolution of his conviction that the Mosaic Law is the authoritative word of God, a word that has nonetheless been interpreted by the Spirit in unforeseen ways. Under the transforming image of this eschatological Spirit, the Mosaic Law is assimilated by the gospel.[46]

The essential points of Thielman's argumentation in his book appeared the previous year in more summary form within his article "Law" in *Dictionary of Paul and His Letters.*[47] Here Thielman surveys the passages relevant to Jewish Law in 1 and 2 Thessalonians,[48] 1 Corinthians, 2 Corinthians, Galatians, Philippians, and Romans. Following T. J. Deidun,[49] Thielman points out that, despite the lack of the word *nomos* (Law) in the Thessalonian correspondence, the use of the phrase "'the church' of the Thessalonians in God the Father and the Lord Jesus Christ" (1 Thes 1:1), as well as the portrayal of the Judean Christians as "the churches of God" (2 Thes 2:14), has connections with Israel's status as the "church of God" when they assembled to receive the Law at Mt. Sinai (Dt 4:9–14, 9:10, 10:4, 18:16; the Greek word *ekklesia* translates the Hebrew *qahal,* which in English can be rendered "church" or "assembly."). Likewise, the "specific precepts" (1 Thes 4:2) that Paul gives them distinguish them from "the Gentiles who do not know God" (1 Thes 4:7–9) and thus echo the holiness language of Leviticus and Jeremiah. "Both old covenant and new emphasize sanctity through behavior and for identical reasons; but the new covenant, unlike the old, is not ethnically determined."[50]

As in the Thessalonian correspondence, Thielman maintains, much of what 1 Corinthians has to say regarding sanctity and ethics presupposes a stance toward the Law in a context free of polemic against the Law. The Corinthian Christians are also "the church of God...set apart in Christ Jesus" (1 Cor 1:2), "God's temple" (1 Cor 3:17) who should be distinguished from the Gentiles by their abstention from sexual immorality (1 Cor 5:1) and by separating themselves from those who refuse to shun immorality (1 Cor 5:10–13). 1 Corinthians also reflects a concern to reject idolatry and an awareness of the covenant history of Israel, especially in 1 Corinthians 10, which claims for Christians the promised eschatological inheritance of Israel. A positive attitude toward the Law surfaces in 1 Corinthians 7:19, where the expression "keeps the commands of God" is equivalent in the literature of Paul's day to "observing the Jewish Law." In 1 Corinthians 9:8–9 and 14:21, Paul invokes the Mosaic Law, respectively, to support an argument and to prove a point, and in 2 Corinthians 9:19–23 Paul contends that he is not "outside the Law but within the Law of Christ." How then can Paul, in 1 Corinthians 7, assert that circumcision, one of the Law's most conspicuous commands, did not matter? Here Thielman appears to agree with Dunn that what Paul seems to be rejecting are those parts of the Law that entail Jewish ethnic "identity markers." Nonetheless, this is not a final solution, for in 1 Corinthians 15:56 Paul seems to totally undercut any positive aspect of the Law by associating it with sin and death. How can Paul hold the Law to be an authority in such a context?

A clue to the dilemma must be sought in 2 Corinthians. Here too, Paul appeals to the Law as an authority and guide for the everyday conduct of believers. However, as in 1 Corinthians, one passage seems in flagrant contrast, 2 Corinthians 3:1–18, where once again the Law is linked with sin, death, and condemnation. Thielman suggests that the presence of a similar set of contrasting attitudes in two letters dealing with different situations is a first indication that the supposed contrasts form part of a complex but nonetheless coherent position toward the Law. A second such indication lies in the character of Paul's negative statements against the Law, which should be read against the first-century Jewish conviction that the Law had justly condemned Israel for its transgressions, which resulted in Gentile domination. Paul may be insisting not that every aspect of the Mosaic Law was abolished, but only the Law's just sentence of condemnation: "…since the Mosaic Law was inextricably bound to a period of time in which the boundaries of God's people were virtually identical with the boundaries of the Jewish people and to a time in which God's people labored under a justly pronounced sentence of condemnation, it has come to its divinely appointed end (see esp. 2 Cor 3:13)."[51]

In Galatians, Thielman continues, it is clear that Paul is angrily responding to a situation in which Jewish Christians, probably under pressure from (non-Christian) Jews in Palestine, are attempting to impose requirements on the Gentile Christians regarding observance of circumcision, Jewish holy days, and dietary restrictions. Paul's rejoinder, which is compressed and not easily understandable, nonetheless clearly flows from the central convictions that a new era has dawned and that within it God has established a new covenant with a newly constituted people.

Thus, Paul's discussion of the Law in Galatians moves in two directions. The first, and predominant, is that national identity markers, or "works of the Law," cannot make a person righteous before God both because no one can keep the Law in its entirety, and also because, unlike the promise to Abraham, the Sinai covenant was a temporary measure. The development of this reasoning is accomplished through a variety of metaphors connected in one way or another with the notion of slavery. The second direction consists of remarks in which Paul refers to the Law positively (e.g., Gal 5:14, 6:2). This second aspect should not be surprising, since, for one, examination of the Corinthian correspondence has demonstrated a similar pattern of regarding Mosaic legislation as passé while still referring to the Law positively, and, for another, in neither case does Paul contend that each specific command of the Mosaic Law is obsolete, but rather the code regarded as a whole, with its curses for disobedience and its barriers against Gentiles. Those aspects of the Mosaic Law which are untainted by the temporal nature of the curses and barriers remain valid and are fulfilled by believers who walk in the Spirit (Gal 5:22–23, 6:2).[52]

In Philippians, written, in Thielman's opinion, when Paul's memory of the Galatian controversy was as yet vivid, there is a warning against the same Jewish Christians depicted in the earlier letter, though this group does not at this point pose an active threat to the Christians in Philippi. Paul's brief warning against this group in Philippians 3 provides a serviceable link between his forceful and compact remarks about the Law in Galatians and his more carefully nuanced comments in Romans. In Philippians, as in Galatians, Paul argues that to demand fulfillment of the obsolete requirements of the Mosaic Law is to place confidence in "the flesh," that is, in humanity's inadequate, fallen ability to do God's will (Phil 3:3–4; cf. Gal 2:16). Going beyond the argument in Galatians, Paul maintains that to place confidence in works such as circumcision is to rely on one's own inadequate righteousness rather than on the righteousness that comes from God.

This new twist in the argument relies on two biblical images (not explicitly cited). The first is that of Israel's own inadequate righteousness during the wilderness period, despite which God led them into the promised land (Deut 9:1—10:11). Paul's "own" righteousness, based on this broken Sinaitic covenant, was likewise inadequate. The second image is that of God's mighty and effective action to rescue Israel from exile and restore the people of God to their land and to a peaceful relationship with God, which God describes in Isaiah 46:13 and 51:5–8 as "my righteousness." Paul utilizes this concept in Philippians 3:9 to assert that biblical anticipations of an eschatological display of God's righteousness have at least begun to be fulfilled in Jesus Christ; thus to cling to the inadequate righteousness based on a broken covenant is to put one's trust in "refuse" (Phil 3:8). The relationship between Law, conceived as the Sinaitic covenant, and "righteousness from God" will become a dominant theme in Romans.[53]

Thielman begins his discussion of Romans by providing an overview of the situation that prompted the letter. Paul was about to deliver his collection of relief funds solicited from his predominantly Gentile churches to the Jewish Christians in Jerusalem but was concerned that this offering, on which he had expended considerable energy, would not be well received. Since the Roman church may well have had close ties to that in Jerusalem, and since Acts 21:20–21 indicates that Paul was concerned about what Jewish Christians in Jerusalem had heard about his view of the Law, it is likely that one of his reasons for writing the Letter to the Romans was to rectify misconceptions regarding his view of the Law.

Once again, Paul has both positive and negative things to say about the Law, asserting that "works of the Law" cannot give righteousness, but also that the Law, no longer thought of in terms of the Sinai covenant, can be fulfilled by Christians. However, his critique of the Sinai covenant is articulated from a slightly different perspective, now including an argument against "boasting" or "glorying" in the Law as a singular privilege of the Jewish people. His first point is that knowledge of God's will does not ensure

right standing before God; obedience to God's will is also necessary. Many Gentiles have an awareness of God's power (Rom
1:20), creative activity (Rom 1:25), and moral standard (Rom
1:32), but nonetheless sin against God (Rom 1:21–31) and
receive deserved punishment (Rom 1:24, 26, 28). Jews can expect
a similar divine standard of judgment, which could even envision
that an uncircumcised Gentile who keeps the Law in spirit might
sit in judgment on a Jew who boasts in possession of the Law
without obeying it. The main point of the complex passage
Romans 2:14–29 is that it is useless for Jewish–Christians to
impose on Gentile Christians a standard that historically the Jews
themselves have been incapable of keeping. In Romans 3:9–20
Paul goes further and points out the inability of anyone, Jew or
Gentile, to fully keep the requirements of the Law. Only eschatological help from the covenant-keeping God can provide a remedy, and this remedy has been provided by God in Jesus Christ.

At this point, Thielman believes, Paul has for the most part
made his case, though several "loose threads" remain to be dealt
with. First, Paul answers the objection that he has nullified the
Law, which he believes is God's Word (Rom 3:31), by appealing
not to the covenant with Moses but to the narrative portion of the
Law, particularly to God's covenant with Abraham. Paul maintains that God accounted Abraham as righteous before he was circumcised, and that his subsequent circumcision served only to
seal a covenant already made based on faith. Thus faith, not
"works" of the Mosaic Law, brings righteousness, and Abraham
can be the model for believing Jews as well as believing Gentiles.
Paul makes clear that rather than nullifying the Law, "the righteousness of God" is consistent with the principle of faith that is
found in the Law itself.[54]

A second difficulty is raised in the question of why God gave
the Law, if it gives no advantage to Jews. Paul is careful to point out
that despite his criticisms the Law is not identical with sin (Rom
7:7) but rather is holy, good, spiritual, and righteous (Rom 7:12,
14). It is linked so closely with sin because it demonstrates the evil

transgression that constitutes sin and thus condemns the sinner, and this in three ways: (1) It makes God's will explicit and thus brings knowledge of sin, since people can know God's will and be aware that they have failed to accomplish it (Rom 3:20; 4:15; 5:13; 7:7, 21–23). (2) It manifests the insidiousness of sin by suggesting to fallen humanity ways in which to rebel against God (Rom 7:7–12; cf. 5:20). (3) It enumerates the dire consequences that await those who disobey its commands.

Thus, as in his other letters, Paul can speak clearly of the annulment of the Mosaic Law while at the same time maintaining the Law's authority and its fulfillment among believers. In Romans, however, there is a sharper tension between these two perspectives. The resolution of the tension already apparent in earlier letters—Paul's belief in two covenants, or two laws, one old and another new—appears in Romans 9:30—10:8, where Paul makes clear that the reason most of Israel has not accepted the gospel is because it has continued to cling to a covenant that has been replaced by God's eschatological intervention in Christ. To explain why this clinging could not lead to salvation, Paul quotes Leviticus 18:5, reminding his readers that the Law of Moses promised life only to those who obey it (Rom 10:5), something that neither Israel nor anyone else has been able to accomplish. Further, Paul utilizes the vocabulary of Deuteronomy 9:4 and 30:12, which originally referred to obedience to the Law of Moses, to speak of righteousness by faith in Christ (Rom 10:6–8). The Law, which has reached its climactic end *(telos)* in Christ, can be assumed and remolded in the shape of the new covenant.

Thielman concludes by proposing that if the portrait he has painted of Paul's view of the Law is accurate, "then at its heart was the conviction that the old covenant made with Israel at Sinai had passed away and the new covenant predicted by Jeremiah and Ezekiel had come."[55] This change was required for two reasons: (1) No individual could keep the provisions of the old covenant, and Israel had demonstrated this on a national level as well. (2) Once the covenant was broken, Israel utilized the Law to set up barriers between itself and the Gentiles, and to some extent these became a point of pride and false security. While the new covenant retained the formal structure of the old, including its notion of separation between those within and those outside, the barriers were no longer national, but Spirit-directed, and in many practical instances often coincided with particulars of the old covenant. The new covenant, written on the heart, could be kept by those who were led by the Spirit.

While this means that Paul's view of the Law was to a great extent discontinuous with the view of many of his Jewish contemporaries, Thielman cautions that the element of discontinuity should not be overstressed. Paul was neither an aberration within the Judaism of his day, nor as muddle-headed as Räisänen makes him out to be. His convictions remain consistent from his earliest correspondence to his latest, from his most irenic to his most polemical. His view of the Law was not an expedient of the moment, but rather "a complex and carefully considered position, worthy of the most painstaking study and the deepest theological reflection."[56]

Law in Paul and the Jesus Tradition: David Wenham

David Wenham has come to similar conclusions regarding the consistency of Paul's teaching on the Law, apparently independently of Sloan and Thielman. In *Paul: Follower of Jesus or Founder of Christianity?,* his primary intention is to demonstrate the theological continuity between the Jesus tradition and the letters of Paul; in the process the picture of Paul that emerges includes the aspect of consistency in regard to the apostle's view of the Law.

From an eschatological perspective that understands salvation in Christ in the context of fulfillment of Old Testament promises, Wenham relates Paul's terminology of "righteousness" and "reconciliation" to Jesus' use of "kingdom of God" language. He views righteousness as an important Pauline category of thought, though not necessarily as its unique center. According to Wenham, justification/righteousness language has a wide range of meaning in Paul, but the overarching notion is that of God's eschatological righteousness breaking into history and into human lives through Jesus Christ. A narrow interpretation of Pauline justification as the exoneration of individual sinners by the divine judge because of the work of Christ reflects an experience of personal guilt, reinforced by modern individualism, and does justice neither to Paul's view rooted in Old Testament hope nor to the kingdom teaching of Jesus.[57]

Regarding the Law, Wenham argues that the ethical vision of Jesus was that of a return to the perfection of creation. There is at least some evidence to suggest that he interpreted his mission in terms of the new covenant of Jeremiah 3:31–34, which speaks of the written Law being superseded by the Law written on the heart. It is possible, though difficult to prove conclusively, that Jesus viewed the ritual law as a temporary dispensation both fulfilled and made redundant with the coming of the kingdom through his own sacrificial death. Nonetheless, the combination of ethical rigor, openness to sinners, and ritual liberalism in the gospel portraits of Jesus does make sense in such a context, and Matthew 11:12–13/Luke 16:16 state that the Law and the prophets were in effect *until* the time of John the Baptist, with the implication that the age of the Law and the prophets is giving way to the age of the kingdom.[58]

Turning again to Paul, Wenham points out that though the dispute between Paul and his opponents regarding imposition of the Law on Gentiles was originally a question of ritual, the ethical question inevitably flowed from it because the Law also made ethical demands. Paul needed to defend himself against the charge that his version of the Gospel was undermining ethical conduct. In demonstrating Paul's overall consistency on the issue of the Law, Wenham makes four major points:

1. Paul, even as a Christian, perceived God's plan of salvation within an Old Testament framework and viewed Jesus from within that context; he thus continued to recognize the Law of Moses as God-given, holy, and good.

2. Paul experienced in his own life the "failure" of the Law, discovering himself to be in opposition to the Messiah. Similarly, he saw such failure both in the history of Israel and in the attitudes of those of his Jewish contemporaries who did not believe in Jesus as Messiah. This was not the fault of the Law, but the result of its coming under the sway of sin; nonetheless, this cannot be an accident that God failed to foresee, so Paul concludes that the Mosaic Law was never intended to produce righteousness and life, but rather to point out sin and convict sinners.

3. Paul viewed the coming of Christ as a turning point in history, the end of the era of the Law and the inauguration of the possibility of living in freedom as God's adopted children.

4. The freedom that Paul envisioned and experienced was a freedom into relationship with Christ, release to a new life in Christ and the Spirit; thus its result is not ethical anarchy, but rather newness of life, not only as a possibility, but as an ethical imperative based on the indicative of being in Christ.

Within the Jesus tradition, Wenham acknowledges, the view of the Law is both less complex and less negative than in Paul. Nonetheless, he points out five areas of overlap:

1. While the teaching of Jesus does not indict the Law as an ally of sin, it does contain a negative assessment of Pharisaic righteousness; such righteousness is found seriously wanting, and Jesus demands a much higher righteousness, more suitable to the kingdom of God.

2. The higher righteousness demanded by Jesus is not depicted as something that can be achieved by superior law keeping; rather, it is presented both as a human impossibility and as an option for the sinners and spiritually poor, who are conspicuous failures by Pharisaic standards.

This paradox is to be explained in terms of Jesus' conviction that a new era is dawning: The age of the Law and the prophets gives way to the effective and powerful rule of God and the new covenant. This implies that the previous era was not notably successful in terms of righteousness.

3. Jesus' comments on divorce, which hark back to creation principles as opposed to Mosaic concessions, hint in the direction of Paul's views of the Law and new creation.

4. Paul and the Jesus tradition agree in referring to the Law as being "fulfilled" in the mission and salvation of Jesus.

5. Jesus' liberalism toward the ritual law, as well as his vision of a new spiritual temple, tend in the direction that Paul eventually took. In particular, the Matthean story of the coin in the fish's mouth (Matt 17:24–27) is very similar to the Pauline position on issues such as food offered to idols (Rom 14:13–23, 1 Cor 8).[59]

Wenham develops his fourth point in more detail in another section of his book. He notes that, in both Romans and Galatians, Paul's exhortations about love begin with the call to love "one another" (Rom 13:8, Gal 5:13) and suggests that Paul may well have been familiar with the tradition behind the "new commandment" in the Johannine writings. One serious possibility for Paul's reference to the "Law of Christ" in Galatians 6:2 is that he is referring to the teaching of Jesus; it seems likely that both Paul and John know the same tradition, which emphasized that "love one another" was *Jesus'* commandment. Though the Synoptic Gospels suggest that Jesus challenged narrow and/or exclusive definitions of love, they also imply that Jesus spoke of disciples having special responsibility toward one another. This is particularly evident in Matthew 18/Mark 9:42–50/Luke 17:1–4, where there is some reason to believe the evangelists have derived material from independent traditions.

Additionally, Wenham points to traces of Paul's familiarity with Jesus' teaching on love within the community in 1 Thessalonians 4:9 and 5:13. Likewise Paul, in common with the Jesus tradition found in the Synoptic Gospels, also exhorts believers to a wider love, as in 1 Thessalonians 3:12 and 5:12, as well as Galatians 6:10, Romans 12:18, and 1 Corinthians 7:15. Paul's references to care for the weak and to humble serving also display links with the Jesus tradition: (1) Paul speaks negatively of people pleasing themselves, acting from selfish ambition, and vain boasting (Rom 15:1; 1 Cor 10:24, 33; Phil 2:3–4, 21), while the Synoptics have Jesus respond to the disciples' desire to be the greatest with negative comments on worldly patterns of leadership. (2) In both traditions, self-glorification is contrasted with an attitude of humble servanthood/slavery (Phil 2:7–9, 1 Cor 9:19, 2 Cor 11:7, Rom 15:8, Matt 20:26–28/Mark 10:43–45, Matt 23:12). (3) In the Pauline texts cited, the apostle specifically relates both his own servant ministry and Christian servanthood in a more general sense to Jesus' own servanthood.[60]

While at times Wenham supports his argumentation with examples from the disputed Paulines, this should not be perceived as a major obstacle to acceptance of his suggestions, since nowhere does his argument depend wholly or even substantially on these references. Some will object that his allusions to the Jesus tradition may well reflect the views of the gospel authors more than that of Jesus himself, but one must read the book in its entirety to determine the degree to which various arguments are convincing.

Restatements and Synthesis: J. D. G. Dunn

J. D. G. Dunn has returned to the topic of Law in the letters of Paul in articles on justification by faith in 1992 and 1997[61] and on the Law as portrayed in Galatians (1993).[62] In 1995 he employed Galatians and Romans as a test case, attempting to answer the question, "Was Paul against the Law?" from textual and situational contexts.[63] In September 1994, he chaired the Third Durham-Tübingen Research Symposium on earliest Christianity and Judaism, held in Durham, which discussed the topic "Paul and the Mosaic Law,"[64] and, in his closing remarks, attempted to identify the possibility of common ground within the discussion.

Dunn's most extensive treatment of the topic occurs in two sections of his recent magisterial study, *The Theology of Paul the Apostle* (1998): The law[65] and Justification by faith.[66] In this work, he takes issue with authors such as M. Bachmann[67] and Stuhlmacher[68] who, he maintains, have misunderstood his initial essay on "works of the law." Dunn insists that he does not, "and never did, claim that 'works of the law' denote only circumcision, food laws, and Sabbath."[69] The phrase has reference to all that the Law requires, but in a context where Israel's relationship with other nations was at issue, particular aspects such as circumcision would naturally receive more emphasis than others, just as in an intra-Jewish context the Qumran sect focused on issues such as purity and sacrifice.[70]

Dunn's discussion of the role of the Law within Paul's indictment of human weakness and transgression is summarized in six major theses:

1. The Law's role is to define sin, bring it to awareness as transgression, and condemn that transgression; in a more implicit way, it fulfills the same function for Gentiles, especially through conscience. This role of the Law is largely unaffected by discussion of its other functions.
2. The Law had a unique relationship with Israel, functioning as protector and disciplinarian from Moses to Christ. This function was temporary, but it was not the Law's only function, and thus the coming of Christ does not mean the abolition of the Law *in toto.*
3. Israel was unable to perceive the temporary character of this function of the Law, as reflected in its ongoing assumption of privileged relationship with God based on its having been given the Law of God.
4. The Law's primary function was to give direction to Israel's living and to make clear the terms on which its covenant status and life were to be preserved.

5. The Law is utilized by the power of sin to enmesh the human weakness of the flesh.

6. The Law as ally of the powers of sin and death should not be understood as itself a cosmic power. The surrender to the power of sin and death may be temporary; God's purpose may have been to exhaust the power of sin in death. The triumph of the Law may be that it converts death from final judgment on the sinner to the final destruction of sin itself.[71]

Summary

The authors in this chapter have been presented in somewhat more detail because in general they take a much more comprehensive approach to the question of Paul and the Law and, as well, because they draw attention to aspects that have received little or no attention before. How well they will convince other scholars of their proposals remains to be seen.

6
The New Center?

Along with a growing attempt to demonstrate that Paul's view of the Law is essentially consistent, there is emerging an increasing consensus that justification by faith alone can no longer be considered the center of Paul's theology. In his 1990 monograph, *Paul and the Jewish Law,* Peter J. Tomson follows in the line of earlier scholars such as Wrede and Baur who challenged the centrality of the Law polemic in Paul. Tomson's wide-ranging but close study of the relevant texts on Law in the letters of Paul, a historical examination of the *halakha* manifested in Paul's letters, is based on three postulates: (1) Paul's historical background was in the Judaism expressed in ancient Jewish sources. (2) The Law retained a practical function for Paul. (3) The governing concern of Paul was not the Law polemic.[1]

Although justification by faith is no longer so universally recognized as the core of Paul's theology, precisely what does constitute the "new center" of Paul's thought is still a matter of discussion. Dunn has even questioned whether "center" is the most adequate term, preferring to speak of a "fulcrum" or "pivot point."[2] Sanders, in *Paul and Palestinian Judaism* (1977), identifies two primary convictions that ruled Paul's life: (1) that Jesus Christ is Lord, that in him God provided for the salvation of all who believe; (2) that he, Paul, was called to be the apostle to the Gentiles.[3] C. J. A. Hickling (1978), while essentially agreeing with Sanders, believes that a necessary addition is the realization that in Christ God has already accomplished a decisive and final transformation of time.[4]

A Christological Core

A number of scholars before and after Sanders have held and continue to hold some variation of the notion that Christ is the center of Paul's theology. For Lucien Cerfaux (1951), who anticipated much of the modern discussion on Paul, Christ as Son of God is the center of Paul's religious thought; thus, what is stressed is the divinity of Christ and his union with God, so that Christ and God constitute one principle of activity.[5] However, Joseph Plevnik contends that a weakness in Cerfaux's argumentation on this point is his heavy reliance on Ephesians and Colossians, which are among the disputed Paulines.[6] Nonetheless, it seems to me that a good case could be made for Cerfaux's proposal based on the undisputed Paulines. Joseph Fitzmyer, a Jesuit scholar and one of the deans of Catholic New Testament scholarship, has consistently maintained that the key concept in Pauline theology is "christocentric soteriology."[7]

Reconciliation, Death, and Resurrection

Ralph P. Martin criticizes the proposals of both Cerfaux and Fitzmyer as being either too narrow or too vague. Martin has for some time advocated the theme of reconciliation as a central category, though he has not found many supporters, probably because, as he acknowledges, reconciliation terminology is not very frequent in Paul.[8] Another difficulty is that part of Martin's argumentation is based on passages from the disputed Paulines.

As early as 1970, Rudolf Schnackenburg had contended that the twofold event of Jesus' death and resurrection is the source of Paul's christology.[9] Plevnik notes that the death and resurrection of Christ, from the perspective of its saving significance, is a principal notion with regard to justification by faith or participation in Christ, as well as a constant theme occurring in each of Paul's letters. Yet, Plevnik hesitates to identify it as the center, viewing it rather as part, albeit an important part, of the Christ-event.[10] Richard B. Gaffin, Jr. (1978) argues that the theme of the resurrection governs the totality of Paul's theology,[11] while for Alister E. McGrath (1993), it is the cross that is the center of Paul's proclamation of the Gospel.[12] Käsemann asserts that the cross is "the central and in a sense the only theme of Christian theology...the ground and test of Christology."[13] Dunn at one point identifies the cross as "the fulcrum point, the central soteriological moment,"[14] but hastens to add: "If the cross of Jesus stands at the center of Paul's theology, so also does the resurrection of Jesus."[15] At one point Dunn stresses the centrality of Jesus' resurrection for Paul, specifically as *God's* act,[16] but he can also refer to Paul's conversion as the fulcrum point or hinge on which all of Paul's theology turned, and the encounter with the risen Christ as that which formed that fulcrum/hinge.[17]

Eschatology/Apocalyptic

Silva (1996), though inclined to believe that there is a clear center to Paul's thought, recognizes the difficulty of identifying such a center. Nonetheless, he maintains that Paul is a logical, coherent thinker.[18] While Silva believes that Paul's teaching on justification functions as a "conceptual adhesive" that helps to make sense of a great deal of Paul's teaching, he seems at one point more inclined to view the topic of eschatology as fundamental. He notes that early scholars such as Geerhardus Vos, who described the mind of Paul as "highly doctrinal and synthetic,"[19] and Albert Schweitzer, who held a similar opinion,[20] were both much absorbed by the topic of Paul's eschatology.

More recently, both Herman N. Ridderbos (1975)[21] and J. Christiaan Beker (1980)[22] have argued for a comprehensiveness in

Paul's thought as a whole, not simply concerning the topic of Law and, though there are points of difference between them, both utilize eschatology as a central organizing principle. Ridderbos finds a "point of departure for an adequate approach to the whole of Paul's thought in the *redemptive-historical, eschatological character of Paul's proclamation,*" but he nonetheless recognizes the divergent opinions on this "eschatological character," citing Beda Rigaux's reference to "eschatology and eschatologies."[23]

Beker prefers to refer to a "coherent center" of Paul's theology, rather than to a "core" of Paul's theology. It should be pointed out that Beker more predominantly employs the term *apocalyptic* than *eschatology*. While some scholars use these terms virtually as synonyms, others would insist on a distinction, utilizing *eschatology* in a wider sense as referring to anything having to do with the end-time, and *apocalyptic* in a narrower sense, since it is also associated with a specific literary genre of ancient Jewish (and some Jewish-Christian) writing that made use of stock themes and images, such as the final trumpet. (For the rare Pauline utilization of these literary features, see 1 Thes 4:16–17 and 1 Cor 15:51–52.) The apocalyptic perspective, in this strict sense, views the world as essentially corrupt. Humans can do nothing to change this situation, so the task of believers is to remain steadfast and await the action of God. The term *realized eschatology* is frequently employed to indicate that with the coming of Christ the final triumph of the reign of God has already begun, though it remains to be *fully* realized. (The Gospel of John is often said to exhibit a greater degree of realized eschatology than the Synoptic Gospels.) Rarely or never, however, does one encounter the term *realized apocalyptic*. Dunn criticizes "a continuing lack of clarity as to the meaning and appropriate use of the term" *(apocalyptic).*[24] Attempts at further definition have been made by R. E. Sturm[25] and R. B. Matlock.[26]

In the preface to the first paperback edition of *Paul the Apostle* (1984), Beker justifies his practice of reducing apocalyptic to the three motifs of historical dualism, universal-cosmic scope, and imminent expectation of the world's end and explains his preference for *apocalyptic* rather than *eschatological.* At one point, Beker perceives his claim of an apocalyptic center to be in danger. Discerning a virtual absence of reference to Christ's resurrection in Galatians, he expresses a concern that Galatians threatens to undo what he has posited as the coherent center of Paul's thought: "...the apocalyptic coordinates of the Christ-event that focus on the imminent triumph of God....Because the Christocentric focus of Galatians pushes Paul's theocentric apocalyptic theme to the periphery, Galatians cannot serve as the central and normative guide for all Paul's letters and theology."[27]

Silva's reading of a thoroughgoing eschatological perspective in Galatians leads him to take issue with Beker on this point. Silva maintains that it is precisely because this letter grounds the future triumph of God's righteousness in a carefully developed view of realized eschatology that it provides a central guide for Paul's apocalyptic outlook.[28]

Plevnik asserts that Beker's view omits key elements of Paul's understanding of Christ that are not mediated by an apocalyptic framework. These include: (1) Christ's filial relationship with God, which must take into account his role as the pre-existing agent of creation and salvation, as well as his being "in the form of God" (Phil 2:6); (2) Christ's inclusive and representative role, which is attested in conjunction with the universal significance of his death and resurrection; (3) the believer's being conformed to Christ, affirmed in connection with the parousia of Christ; (4) the believer's present participation in Christ.[29]

The Need for Criteria

Despite Silva's assertion that eschatology can be regarded as the center of Paul's theology, he also remarks that it is quite possible to argue convincingly that any one of a dozen doctrines functions as a center.[30] Ralph Martin[31] understands Joseph Plevnik as apparently coming to a similar conclusion in "The Center of

Paul's Theology" (1989) when Plevnik remarks near the end of his survey:

> Any center of Pauline theology must therefore include *all* these components of the apostle's gospel: his understanding of Christ and of God, his understanding of God's salvific action through Christ, involving the Easter event and its implications, the present lordship, the future coming of Christ, and the appropriation of salvation. The center is thus not any *single* aspect of Christ, or of God's action through Christ, but rather the whole and undivided richness and mystery of Christ and the Father's saving purpose through his Son.[32]

Though earlier (1982) John Reumann had maintained the traditional Lutheran position of the centrality of justification in Paul as well as in the New Testament in general,[33] more recently (1991) he has identified at least sixteen themes that have been proposed by various scholars as candidates for this honor. He does not attempt to argue the case for any one, noting that some are virtually interchangeable, but, because they are interrelated, he suggests that it is in the total complex that the unity of Paul's message can be found.[34] Similarly, C. A. Davis (1995) contends that the coherent heart of Paul's theology is comprised of fourteen core convictions which revolve around Christ's death and resurrection to eschatological life, as well as the Christian's death and resurrection to eschatological life.[35]

Ralph Martin (1993) is dissatisfied with both a "too narrow" approach and solutions such as those of Plevnik and Reumann, which, Martin contends, risk casting the net so widely that almost everything in Paul's preaching has equal significance. Thus, Martin proposes the following criteria for determining whether any candidate adequately fits the description "center of Paul's theology:" (1) Paul's demonstrated awareness of a central affirmation or "cluster" of affirmations that embody his chief message; (2) the role of tradition, including Paul's redaction of it; (3) the extent of Paul's correspondence (limited to the seven letters generally recognized as authentic or including disputed epistles); (4) an attempt to locate what is unique in Paul[36] so that, as Plevnik had earlier remarked, "anything that is derived from something else in Pauline theology is not the center."[37]

Martin offers what he describes as five "patterns" in Paul's theological teaching: God's grace, the cosmos, the cross, the ethical imperative, and Paul's missionary mandate.[38] However, though he claims to derive these from Paul's "generally undisputed letters," he does include Ephesians, Colossians, and 2 Thessalonians, the authenticity of which is disputed by a majority, albeit a relatively slight majority, of scholars. He then goes on to argue that his choice, reconciliation, fulfills all the criteria and also incorporates all the patterns he has discovered, citing E. E. Lemcio as having summed up these categories with the following description: "God [who] sent or raised Jesus. A response towards God brings benefits."[39] Dunn has criticized Martin's proposal on the grounds that reconciliation is one of a number of metaphors that Paul employs in attempting to depict the significance of Christ's death and that Martin runs the risk of taking the metaphor too literally by making this one metaphor normative for all the others.[40]

Christocentric Soteriology

I have recently suggested that if one were to seek a consistent core of Pauline theology, it might not be far from wrong to find it expressed in Philippians 3:8: "Christ Jesus my Lord."[41] Ultimately I do not believe that this is very different from the proposal made more than thirty years ago and consistently championed by Fitzmyer: christocentric soteriology. Both of these expressions take into account the two inseparable notions that Hengel and Schwemer have expressed in yet another way: "At the center is not immediately and directly the question of the law—or even the phantom of a preaching 'free of the law'—but the basic question of Christian faith down to the present day: who is Christ, and what did he do for us?…At the beginning stands a personal encounter, a being over-whelmed by the crucified and exalted Christ."[42]

If one looks carefully at the proposals of Sanders, Martin, and Plevnik, these two elements—Who is Christ and what did he do for us?—feature prominently. The first primary conviction of Paul identified by Sanders—that Jesus Christ is Lord, that in him God provided for the salvation of all who believe—is virtually equivalent. The second—that Paul was called to be the apostle to the Gentiles—can be derived from the first and is not sufficiently primary to account for all of Paul's thought (see, e.g., 1 Cor 9:20)[43] The theme of eschatology is likewise secondary: If there is no Christ who has come to save us, Paul would never have written to Gentiles on the theme of eschatology. The eschatological aspect depends on the fact that God acts *in Christ.*

Similarly, Martin's theme of reconciliation suffers from his own criticism of being too general; it is not reconciliation as such that is central, but *Christ* as the instrument of reconciliation. Reconciliation is a way of describing what *Christ* does for us; basically it is a soteriological category. In addition, the summary of the themes which Martin would like to put under the umbrella of reconciliation ("God [who] sent or raised Jesus. A response towards God brings benefits."[44]) in essence also answers the two questions: Who is Christ?—the one sent by God and raised by God; What does he do for us?—he brings God's benefits to those who respond.

The comment of Hengel and Schwemer, "At the beginning stands a personal encounter, a being overwhelmed by the cruci-fied and exalted Christ,"[45] is effectively echoed by Dunn,[46] who maintains that if the imagery of "center" still has relevance for a subject like theology, then Christ must be regarded as the center of Paul's theology or, using Beker's terminology, Christ has to be seen as that which gives coherence to Paul's theological, mission-ary, and pastoral enterprise:[47]

> The centrality of Christ, as showing what God is like, as defining God's Spirit, as the channel of Israel's blessing for

the nations, as demonstrating what obedience to Torah means, as the light which illumines Israel's scriptures, as embodying the paradigm of creation and consummation, as the focus of all sacramental significance, as determining the personal and corporate identity of Christians, as the image to which the salvation process conforms, is simply inescapable in the theology of Paul the apostle.[48]

The final sentence in the passage quoted earlier from Plevnik sounds very similar: "The center is thus not any *single* aspect of Christ, or of God's action through Christ, but rather the whole and undivided richness and mystery of Christ and the Father's saving purpose through his Son."[49] Nonetheless, there is a major difference. The first point of Plevnik's criticism of Beker likewise applies to Dunn. For Plevnik, Christ's filial relationship with God must take into account his role as the preexisting agent of creation and salvation, as well as his being "in the form of God" (Phil 2:6).[50] Dunn is resistant to speaking of Christ's preexistence, except in a very qualified sense, and he interprets Christ's being "in the form of God" in a minimalist way.[51]

It appears to me that Plevnik's description comes very close to Fitzmyer's category of christocentric soteriology. In discussing Fitzmyer's suggestion, Plevnik remarks that whether Fitzmyer's proposal is adequate depends on what one puts into the general phrase "christological soteriology." He questions whether it includes God as principal agent and whether it gives Christ sufficient identity as Son of God.[52] I would venture to suggest that while Fitzmyer may not have specifically expanded on the meaning of this suggestion in every instance when he employs it in this context, one could not fail to derive from his writings on Paul over the course of the years a rich and full christocentric soteriology. The discussion of the subject in his recent Anchor Bible commentary on Romans (1993) appears to leave no reason for doubt. He remarks in the beginning that "Paul gives us little by way of ontological christology; he is interested in the functional aspects of christology, in what Christ Jesus has done for humanity. For this reason Paul's teaching is best characterized as a christocentric soteriology."[53] Nonetheless, Fitzmyer's discussion does include a definite perception of the filial relation of Jesus to the Father, of the significance of the use of the *Kyrios* (Lord) title for Jesus ("In so using *Kyrios* Paul acknowledged along with the rest of the early church that the risen Jesus was on a par with Yahweh of the OT...."[54]), that Jesus was preexistent, even that, in Romans 9:5, Paul may very well be using the title *theos* (God) for Christ, and that Romans clearly manifests a view of Paul's Gospel as one that reveals God's christocentric power.[55]

If Martin would somewhat modify his proposal in the form of the statement that God was, *in Christ,* reconciling the world to God (2 Cor 5:19), it might be considered virtually equivalent, as Fitzmyer has pointed out that "reconciliation" and "salvation" are essentially different perspectives on the same subject, the effects of the Christ-event, which is also portrayed in the images of justification, expiation, redemption, freedom, new creation, sanctification, glorification, and, possibly, pardon.[56] In Dunn's language, these are different metaphors expressing the same reality. The difficulty with utilizing any one of these terms is that though they are more or less synonymous, they are not necessarily coterminous. For example, in a study of sin and righteousness in 2 Corinthians 5:21, the German exegete and Leuven professor Reimund Bieringer has concluded that in this passage "being made righteous" is a parallel expression to "being reconciled." In this specific case, the need for "reconciliation" terminology is dictated by Paul's desire to use an imperative in 5:20.[57] However, whether either of these terms can be utilized everywhere as a virtual equivalent of "salvation" is somewhat more problematic. In the related passage Romans 5:9–10, reconciliation and justification appear to be used synonymously, both referring to a present reality, while salvation is clearly expressed in future terms. *Soteriology* seems to be a better umbrella term to express the whole complex of what Christ does for us because it can include present experiences that lead to the eschatological accomplishment.

My citation from Philippians 3:9, "Christ Jesus my Lord" is another way of conveying the christological and soteriological dimensions of Paul's theology and, in addition, it evokes the personal appropriation of the Lordship of Jesus on the part of Paul. As I have expressed it earlier:

> Believing in Christ and confessing him as Lord, which lead to righteousness and salvation (Rom 10:9–10), is more than believing that Christ rose from the dead and that he has won righteousness and salvation for us by his obedience. It is, as well, the recognition that the obedience of Christ has this salvific character *precisely because of his unique relationship with God.* The obedience of Christ is thus in a totally different category than the obedience of Abraham or any other holy person.[58]

Ultimately, for Paul, what Christ does for us is only possible because of who Christ is, the one in whom "every one of God's promises is a 'Yes'" (2 Cor 1:20, *NRSV*).

Postscript

As this manuscript is being prepared for publication, delegates of the Roman Catholic Church and the Lutheran World Federation are planning to meet in Augsburg, Germany, on the weekend of October 30–31, 1999 to sign a joint statement intended to clarify differences unresolved in the 1998 "Joint Declaration on the Doctrine of Justification." The following thanksgiving prayer for this event by the Lutheran Bishop of the Southeast Michigan Synod, Robert A. Rimbo (ELCA),[1] seems a fitting way to conclude this discussion.

We Thank You, Gracious God
Gracious God, Lord of the Church:
We thank you for all the gifts you give us.
For your servants in this and every age
who have given witness to your love,
we thank you, gracious God.
For visionary leaders who continue to hold to the hope
that one day your Church's sad divisions will cease,
we thank you, gracious God.
For those who guide us in the way you would have us go,
who sign in our stead this historic document
celebrating a common understanding among diverse people,
we thank you, gracious God.
For renewers of your Church in every time and place

who have held to the centrality of your gospel of justification
we thank you, gracious God.
For the promise of a new day
when barriers will become bridges,
we thank you, gracious God.
For the times you give us
to celebrate our unity and our diversity,
we thank you, gracious God.
We thank you, gracious God,
that you have made us your people
through our baptism into Christ.
Continue to work among us and through us,
that your one Church will bear your creative and redeeming Word
to all the world.
We ask this through our Lord Jesus Christ
who lives and reigns with you and the Holy Spirit,
God forever.
    Amen.

—Robert A. Rimbo

Notes

Introduction

1. Joseph Plevnik, *What Are They Saying About Paul?* (New York/Mahwah, N.J.: Paulist, 1986), pp. 55–76.

2. William Wrede, *Paul* (Lexington, Ky.: American Library Association Committee on Reprinting, 1962 [1908]).

3. E. P. Sanders, "Patterns of Religion in Paul and Rabbinic Judaism: A Holistic Method of Comparison," *HTR* 66 (1973): 455–78; *Paul and Palestinian Judaism: A Comparison of Patterns of Religion* (London/Philadelphia, Pa.: SCM/Fortress, 1977); *Paul, the Law and the Jewish People* (Philadelphia, Pa./London: Fortress/SCM, 1983/1985).

4. James D. G. Dunn, "The New Perspective on Paul," *BJRL* 65 (1983): 94–122.

5. Donald A. Hagner, "Paul and Judaism: The Jewish Matrix of Early Christianity: Issues in the Current Debate," *BBR* 3 (1993): 111–30.

6. C. H. Cosgrove, "The Church *with and for* Israel: History of a Theological Novum before and after Barth," *PerspRelStud* 22 (1995): 259–78.

7. For a more detailed presentation of Luther's views see Francis Watson, *Paul, Judaism and the Gentiles: A Sociological Approach*, SNTSMS 56 (Cambridge/London/New York/Melbourne: Cambridge University, 1986), pp. 2–4 and Stephen Westerholm, *Israel's Law and the Church's Faith: Paul and His Recent Interpreters* (Grand Rapids, Mich.: Eerdmans, 1988), pp. 3–12.

8. For the main lines of Baur's critique see F. Watson, *Paul, Judaism and the Gentiles*, pp. 10–12.

9. Wrede, *Paul*; for a more detailed survey of Wrede, see Westerholm, *Israel's Law*, pp. 16–22.

10. Krister Stendahl, "The Apostle Paul and the Introspective Conscience of the West," *HTR* 56 (1963): 199–215. See also Stendahl's more recent work, *Paul Among Jews and Gentiles* (Philadelphia, Pa.: Fortress, 1976).

11. E. P. Sanders, *Paul and Palestinian Judaism*, p. 505.

12. J. Christiaan Beker, "Paul the Theologian: Major Motifs in Pauline Theology," *Int* 43 (1989): 352–65, p. 361.

13. J. H. Houlden, *Paul's Letters from Prison*, PNTC (Middlesex/Baltimore: Penguin, 1970), pp. 96–102.

14. John Reumann, *"Righteousness" in the New Testament: "Justification" in the United States Lutheran-Roman Catholic Dialogue*, with responses by Joseph A. Fitzmyer and Jerome D. Quinn (Philadelphia, Pa./New York: Fortress/Paulist, 1982), pp. 61–63.

15. For a detailed argumentation of this point, see Veronica Koperski, "The Meaning of ΔΙΚΑΙΟΣΥΝΗ in Philippians 3:9," *The Ministry of the Word: Essays in Honor of Prof. Dr. Raymond F. Collins*, Joseph A. Selling, ed., *LS* 20 (1995): 147–69, 154–68.

16. Joachim Gnilka, *Der Philipperbrief*, HTKNT 10/3 (Freiburg/Basel/Vienna: Herder, 1968), pp. 194–95.

17. *Paul and Palestinian Judaism*, p. 506.

18. Peter T. O'Brien, *The Epistle to the Philippians: A Commentary on the Greek Text*, NIGTC (Grand Rapids, Mich.: Eerdmans, 1991), p. 416.

19. P. F. M. Zahl, "A New Source for Understanding German Theology: Käsemann, Bultmann, and the 'New Perspective on Paul,'" *SewTheolRev* 39 (1996): 413–22.

Chapter 1

1. Rudolf Bultmann, *Theologie des Neuen Testaments*, 1, NTG (Tübingen: J. C. B. Mohr, 1948), p. 280 (there is no change in ⁸1980, p. 285, §30,3); ET: *Theology of the New Testament*, 1 (London: SCM,

1968), p. 285. This position is reiterated in Rudolf Bultmann, "ΔΙΚΑΙΟΣΥΝΗ ΘΕΟΥ," *JBL* 83 (1964): 12–16, esp. p. 13.

2. Karl Barth, *Erklärung des Philipperbriefes*, 6th ed. (Zollikon: Evangelischer Verlag, 1947), pp. 99–103. While this edition of Barth's commentary was published in 1947, the lectures on which it is based go back to 1926–27.

3. Wilhelm Michaelis, *Der Brief des Paulus an die Philipper*, THKNT 11 (Leipzig: A Deichert, 1935), p. 57.

4. Gerhard Friedrich, *Die Brief an die Galater, Epheser, Philipper, Kolosser, Thessalonicher und Philemon*, NTD 8 (Göttingen: Vandenhoeck & Ruprecht, ¹⁴1976), p. 161.

5. *Theologie* 1, p. 280; "ΔΙΚΑΙΟΣΥΝΗ ΘΕΟΥ," p. 13; ET, p. 285.

6. *Theologie* 1, pp. 266–75, §28 and 29; ET, pp. 270–79. "End-time" can be viewed from either a future perspective, the time when the reign of God in Christ will overcome all opposition, or from a present perspective, since the coming of Christ has already, in a sense, initiated the end-time.

7. Jacobus J. Müller, *The Epistles of Paul to the Philippians and to Philemon* (Grand Rapids, Mich.: Eerdmans, ⁴1970 [= ¹1950]), pp. 114–15.

8. Josef Ernst, *Die Briefe an die Philipper, an Philemon, an die Kolosser, an die Epheser*, RNT (Regensburg: Friedrich Pustet, ⁶1974), p. 98: "An die Stelle der Eigenleistung ist das Gnadengeschenk Gotte getreten."

9. Ralph P. Martin, *The Epistle of Paul to the Philippians* (London: Tyndale, 1963), p. 148.

10. D. E. H. Whiteley, *The Theology of St Paul* (Oxford: Blackwell, 1964), pp. 163–64.

11. Günter Klein, "Individualgeschichte und Weltgeschichte bei Paulus," *EvTh* 24 (1964): 126–65 and "Sündenverständis und theologia crucis bei Paulus," *Theologia crucis—signum crucis*, Erich Dinkler and Carl Andressen, eds. (Tübingen: Mohr, 1979), pp. 249–82.

12. Hans Hübner, *Law in Paul's Thought*, James Greig, trans. (Edinburgh: T. & T. Clark, 1984), p. 151, based on *das Gesetz bei Paulus* (Göttingen: Vandenhoeck & Ruprecht, 1978); see also pp. 55–57, 63–65, 136–37.

13. John Chrysostom, "Homilies on Galatians," NPNF, 13, Philip

Schaff, ed. (Grand Rapids, Mich.: Eerdmans, 1979), pp. 1–48, pp. 26–27.

14. The views of Wilckens are discussed in chapter 2 below.

15. J. Drane, *Paul: Libertine or Legalist?* (London: SPCK, 1975), pp. 61–77, 132–36.

16. James Hardy Ropes, "'Righteousness' and 'The Righteousness of God' in the Old Testament and in St. Paul," *JBL* 22 (1903): 211–27.

17. F. C. Synge, *Philippians and Colossians: Introduction and Commentary*, 2d ed., Torch Bible Commentaries (London: SCM, 1958 [¹1951]), p. 42. Synge never mentions Bultmann by name.

18. Ibid.; in support Synge cites passages from Isaiah and also refers to Norman H. Snaith, *The Distinctive Ideas of the Old Testament* (London: Epworth, ⁴1950 [¹1944]).

19. Lucien Cerfaux, *Le Christ dans la théologie de saint Paul*, LD 6 (Paris: Les Éditions du Cerf, 1951). ET: *Christ in the Theology of St. Paul*, Geoffrey Webb and Adrian Walker, trans. (New York: Herder & Herder, 1959).

20. F. W. Beare, *A Commentary on the Epistle to the Philippians*, 2d ed., BNTC (London: Adam & Charles Black, 1969), p. 118.

21. Ibid., p. 121.

22. Ibid.; for the entire discussion see pp. 117–22. Beare refers to G. Schenck's article, "Righteousness" (p. 53) in volume 4 of *Bible Key Words* (London: A. & C. Black, 1949–65), a series that was discontinued when Kittel's *TWNT* began to be available in English translation (as *TDNT*). Beare does not cite German authors in his discussion of righteousness, though he refers to Bultmann and Käsemann elsewhere.

23. Ernst Käsemann, "Gottesgerechtigkeit bei Paulus," *ZTK* 58 (1961): 367–78, p. 367. The reference to Philippians 3:9 is simply the starting point for the discussion, and Käsemann does not return to it.

24. Ernst Käsemann, "The Righteousness of God in Paul," *New Testament Questions of Today,* New Testament Library (London: SCM, 1969), pp. 168–82, pp. 170–71.

25. Ibid., pp. 171, 175. Cf. Cerfaux, *Christ*, pp. 297–98, 311–12, 318–19.

26. *New Testament Questions*, p. 172.

27. Ibid., pp. 176–78.

28. Cerfaux, *Christ in the Theology of St. Paul*, pp. 230–43, 319.

29. Manfred T. Brauch, "Perspectives on 'God's righteousness' in recent German discussion," in Sanders, *Paul and Palestinian Judaism*, pp. 523–42.

30. Günter Klein, "Righteousness in the New Testament," *IDB-Sup*, pp. 750–52.

31. Richard B. Hays, "Psalm 143 and the Logic of Romans 3," *JBL* 99 (1980) 109–15, p. 111.

32. Nils Alstrup Dahl, "Romans 3:9: Text and Meaning," *Paul and Paulinism: Essays in Honor of C. K. Barrett*, Morna D. Hooker and S. G. Wilson, eds. (London: SPCK, 1982), pp. 184–204.

33. Jouette M. Bassler, *Divine Impartiality: Paul and a Theological Axiom*, SBLDS 59 (Atlanta, Ga.: Scholars, 1982).

34. David Hall, "Romans 3:1–8 Reconsidered," *NTS* 29 (1983): 183–97.

35. C. H. Cosgrove, "What If Some Have Not Believed? The Occasion and Thrust of Romans 3:1–8," *ZNW* 78 (1987): 90–105, esp. p. 96.

36. John W. Olley, *"Righteousness" in the Septuagint of Isaiah: A Contextual Study*, SBLSCS 8 (Missoula, Mont.: Scholars, 1979), p. 115.

37. Ralph P. Martin, *Philippians*, rev. ed., NCBC (London: Marshall, Morgan & Scott, 1980), p. 131.

38. Ibid., p. 132.

39. J. Christiaan Beker, *Paul the Apostle: The Triumph of God in Life and Thought* (Philadelphia, Pa.: Fortress, 1980), pp. 263–64.

40. Brendan Byrne, "Living Out the Righteousness of God: The Contribution of Rom 6:1—8:13 to an Understanding of Paul's Ethical Presuppositions," *CBQ* 43 (1981): 557–81. p. 558, n. 3.

41. Peter Stuhlmacher, *Gerechtigkeit Gottes bei Paulus*, FRLANT 87 (Göttingen: Vandenhoeck & Ruprecht, 1965), pp. 99–101.

42. On p. 100 (*Gerechtigkeit Gottes*) Stuhlmacher begins by referring to baptism as "analogous" to Paul's Damascus experience, but he goes on to apply baptismal terminology in regard to Paul.

43. J. A. Ziesler, *The Meaning of Righteousness in Paul: A Linguistic and Theological Enquiry* (Cambridge, U.K.: University Press, 1972), pp. 148–151.

44. J. A. Ziesler, *Paul's Letter to the Romans*, TPI New Testament Commentaries (London/Philadelphia, Pa.: SCM/Trinity Press International, 1989) and "Justification by Faith," *Theology* 94 (1991): 188–94.

45. E.g., Stuhlmacher, *Gerechtigkeit Gottes*, p. 101.

46. Martin Dibelius, *An die Thessalonicher I, II, an die Philipper*, 3d, rev. ed., HNT 11 (Tübingen: J. C. B. Mohr, 1937), p. 89.

47. Joachim Gnilka, *Der Philipperbrief*, p. 195.

48. Friedrich, *Philipper*, p. 161.

49. Georg Strecker, *Eschaton und Historie* (Göttingen: Vandenhoeck & Ruprecht, 1979), p. 237.

50. This meaning is accepted by Beare, *Philippians*, p. 120, though he also says it is a level of moral achievement that God (as Judge) will approve.

51. Ziesler, *The Meaning of Righteousness*, p. 149, uses *forgiveness* synonymously with *acceptance* and *justification*. Beare does not employ the term *acceptance*, but does say (p. 120): "The righteousness which proceeds from God rests upon the thought that God has 'justified' him; that is to say, has pronounced him righteous."

52. Ziesler, ibid., p. 149.

53. Beare, p. 120, cites Psalm 32:1–2 and Romans 4:7–8.

54. *The Meaning of Righteousness*, p. 150.

55. The reference to "blamelessness" in 3:6, and the use of the verb "to be found" in v. 8, which "may refer to the Last Judgement" (ibid.).

56. Cf. *The Meaning of Righteousness*, pp. 36–45.

57. *The Meaning of Righteousness*, p. 212.

58. Ibid., pp. 36–43; quotation from p. 42.

59. Ibid., p. 43.

60. Nigel M. Watson, (*The Meaning of Righteousness*), NTS 20 (1973–74): 217–28, p. 219.

61. Ziesler, p. 189, cited on p. 228 of Watson.

62. *The Meaning of Righteousness*, p. 149.

63. R. G. Hamerton-Kelly, "Sacred Violence and the Law of Moses," in *Sacred Violence: Paul's Hermeneutic of the Cross* (Minneapolis, Minn.: Fortress, 1992), pp. 140–60.

64. R. G. Hamerton-Kelly, "Paul's Hermeneutic of the Cross," *Dialog* 32 (1993): 247–54.

65. See the entire issue of *Dialog* 32 (1993), which includes a number of these responses.

66. Neil Elliott, "Paul and the Lethality of the Law," *Foundations and Facets Forum* 9, 3–4 (1993): 237–56; quotation from p. 254.

67. Stanley B. Marrow, Review of Robert G. Hamerton-Kelly, *Sacred Violence: Paul's Hermeneutic of the Cross* (Minneapolis, Minn.: Fortress, 1992), in *CBQ* 56 (1994): 137–38; quotation from p. 138.

Chapter 2

1. E. P. Sanders, "Paul on the Law, His Opponents, and the Jewish People in Philippians 3 and 2 Corinthians 11," *Paul and the Gospels*, Anti-Judaism in Early Christianity 1, SCJ 2, Peter Richardson, ed. (Waterloo, Ontario: Wilfrid Laurier University, 1986), pp. 75–90, p. 79.

2. Synge, *Philippians*, p. 41.

3. Ibid., pp. 41–42.

4. Lanfranc, *Epistola B. Pauli ap. ad Philippenses cum interjectis B. Lanfranci glossulis*, PL 150 (1854), cols. 307–20, esp. 313–16.

5. Augustine, *Contra Faustum libri triginta tres*, CSEL 25, Joseph Zycha, ed. (Prague-Vienna/Leipzig: Tempsky/Freytag, 1891), pp. 249–797, pp. 760–61 (32:1), 767–68 (32:8–9).

6. Hans Joachim Schoeps, *Paul: The Theology of the Apostle in Light of Jewish Religious History* (Philadelphia, Pa.: Westminster, 1961), pp. 171–262.

7. Andrea van Dülmen, *Die Theologie des Gesetzes bei Paulus*, SBM 5 (Stuttgart: Katholisches Bibelwerk, 1968), pp. 174–79, 251–54, esp. pp. 178 and 252.

8. Ulrich Wilckens, "Was heißt bei Paulus: 'Aus Werken des Gesetzes wird kein Mensch gerecht'?" EKKNT 1 (Zürich/Cologne/Neukirchen: Benziger/Neukirchener, 1968), pp. 51–77, pp. 71–72.

9. Ulrich Wilckens, "Zur Entwicklung des paulinischen Gesetzesverständnis," *NTS* 28 (1981–82) 154–90, *Der Brief an die Römer*, EKKNT 6, 3 vols. (Einsiedeln: Benziger, 1978–82).

10. *Paul and Palestinian Judaism*, p. 551.

11. In a similar vein, Johannes Sijko Vos argues that Paul often used a type of rhetorical device employed in both the Jewish and Hellenistic milieu of his day that involved changing the content of terminology either by association or disassociation. Vos uses Romans 3:27–31 and 8:2 as illustrations in Johannes Sijko Vos, "Legen statuimus. Rhetorische Aspekte der Gesetzesdebatte zwischen Juden und Christen,"

Juden und Christen in der Antike, J. van Amersfoort and J. van Oort, eds. (Kampen: Kok, 1990), pp. 44–60, pp. 45–53.

12. *Paul and Palestinian Judaism*, p. 504.

13. Ibid., p. 506.

14. Ibid., p. 495.

15. E. P. Sanders, "Patterns of Religion in Paul and Rabbinic Judaism: A Holistic Method of Comparison," *HTR* 66 (1973): 455–78, pp. 470–71, 477–78; Moisés Silva, *Philippians*, WEC (Chicago: Moody, 1988 [reissued in 1992 by Baker, Grand Rapids, Mich., in the series Baker Exegetical Commentary on the New Testament, as # 11]), pp. 185–89.

16. *Paul, the Law and the Jewish People*, pp. 44–45.

17. For an example of this view see Victor Paul Furnish, *Theology and Ethics in Paul* (Nashville, Tenn./New York: Abingdon, 1968), pp. 137–38.

18. See esp. pp. 419–23, 426–27, 550.

19. *Paul, the Law and the Jewish People*, p. 44.

20. Ibid., pp. 44–45. See also "Paul on the Law," pp. 78–79, where this interpretation is reiterated.

21. Johannes P. Louw and Eugene A. Nida, *Greek-English Lexicon of the New Testament Based on Semantic Domains*, 1 (New York: United Bible Societies, 1988) agree with Rudolf Bultmann, "καυχάομαι," *TWNT* 3, 646–54, esp. 649–53 ("*kauchaomai*," *TDNT* 3, 645–54, esp. 649–52) and "πείθω" *TWNT* 6, 1–12, esp. 5–9 ("*peitho*," *TDNT* 6, 1–11, esp. 4–8) that *kauchaomai* (33.368) and the perfect of *peitho* (31.82), together with their related substantives (33.368, 33.371, 33.372, 25.203, 25.204; 31.82), have the sense of "relying on" (the substantives can designate who or what is relied on; numbers within parentheses are from Louw and Nida). Similarly, W. E. Vine, *An Expository Dictionary of New Testament Words* (Old Tappan, N.J.: Fleming H. Revell, [17]1966), pp. 135–36, 225.

22. Wolfgang Schenk, *Die Philipperbriefe des Paulus* (Stuttgart/Berlin/Cologne/Mainz: W. Kohlhammer, 1984), pp. 280–81.

23. Ibid., pp. 282–83.

24. Ibid., pp. 309–11.

25. Schenk, *Die Philipperbriefe*, pp. 298–302. Robert H. Gundry, "The Moral Frustration of Paul Before His Conversion: Sexual Lust in Romans 7:7–25," *Pauline Studies: Essays Presented to Professor F. F.*

Bruce on His 70th Birthday, Donald A. Hagner and Murray J. Harris, eds. (Exeter/Grand Rapids, Mich.: Paternoster/Eerdmans, 1980), pp. 228–45, p. 234.

26. Jürgen Becker, *Das Heil Gottes*, SUNT 3 (Göttingen: Vandenhoeck & Ruprecht, 1964), p. 125.

27. Herbert Braun, *Gesammelte Studien zum Neuen Testament und seiner Umwelt*, 2d, rev. ed. (Tübingen, J. C. B. Mohr, 1967 [¹1962]), pp. 8–65.

28. Joachim Schüpphaus, *Die Psalmen Salomos*, ALGHJ 7 (Leiden: E. J. Brill, 1977), pp. 83–117, pp. 138–42.

29. *Paul and Palestinian Judaism*, p. 501.

30. Schenk believes the opponents to be Jews who are not Christian, in contrast to the majority of scholars who believe they are Jewish Christians who are attempting to impose circumcision on the Gentile Christians at Philippi.

31. *Die Philipperbriefe*, p. 311.

32. Robert Badenas, *Christ the End of the Law: Romans 10:4 in Pauline Perspective*, JSNTSup 10 (Sheffield: JSOT, 1985).

33. N. T. Wright, *The Climax of the Covenant: Christ and the Law in Pauline Theology* (Minneapolis, Minn.: Fortress, 1992).

34. Steven Richard Bechtler, "Christ the Τέλος of the Law: The Goal of Romans 10:4," *CBQ* 56 (1994): 288–308.

35. C. F. Edgar, "Paul and the Law: A Narrative Analysis of the Pentateuch and Its Significance for Understanding Romans 9:30—10:4," *SewTheolRev* 39 (1996): 269–84.

36. Douglas Moo, "Paul and the Law in the Last Ten Years," *SJT* 40 (1987): 287–307, pp. 302–304; quotation from p. 304.

37. Joseph A. Fitzmyer, *Romans: A New Translation with Introduction and Commentary*, AB 33 (Doubleday: New York/London/Toronto/Sydney/Auckland: 1993), pp. 584–85.

38. Heikki Räisänen, "Legalism and Salvation by the Law. Paul's portrayal of the Jewish religion as a historical and theological problem," *Die Paulinische Literatur und Theologie/The Pauline Literature and Theology*, Skandinavische Beiträge/Scandinavian Contributions, Teologiske Studier 7, Sigfred Pedersen, ed. (Århus/Göttingen: Forlaget Aros/Vandenhoeck & Ruprecht, 1980), pp. 63–83, pp. 68–72, quotation from p. 71.

39. Heikki Räisänen, *Paul and the Law*, WNUT 29 (Tübingen: J. C. B. Mohr, 1983), esp. pp. 162–77.

40. Heikki Räisänen, "Paul's Conversion and the Development of His View of the Law," *NTS* 33 (1987): 404–19, p. 408.

41. "Paul's Conversion," p. 408. Once again, this echoes the thought of Augustine, who also stressed that for pious Jews "blameless" does not necessarily mean "perfect" in Augustine, *De peccatorum meritis et remissione et de baptismo parvulorum ad Marcellinum libri tres*, CSEL 60, C. F. Urba and Joseph Zycha, eds. (Vienna/Leipzig: Tempsky/Freytag, 1913), pp. 1–151, and also *Sermon 169*, SAAHEO 5, cols. 810–11 (CLXIX:6).

42. *Paul and the Law*, p. 106.

43. *Paul, the Law and the Jewish People*, pp. 77, 78, and 80.

44. Ibid., p. 23. Augustine's view, which has recently been restated by several authors, seems more likely. See, e.g., Frank Thielman, *From Plight to Solution: A Jewish Framework for Understanding Paul's View of the Law in Galatians and Romans*, NovTSup 61 (Leiden/New York/Copenhagen/Cologne: E. J. Brill, 1989), pp. 28–45, 110.

45. E.g., Seyoon Kim, *The Origin of Paul's Gospel*, WUNT 2/4 (Tübingen: J. C. B. Mohr, 1981), p. 287.

46. Räisänen, "Paul's Conversion," p. 409.

47. Ibid.

48. Ibid., pp. 409–10.

49. Watson, *Paul, Judaism and the Gentiles*, p. 78.

50. Ibid., pp. 177–78.

51. "Paul's Conversion," p. 410.

52. *Paul, the Law and the Jewish People*, p. 198.

53. *Paul and Palestinian Judaism*, p. 496.

54. "Legalism and Salvation," p. 77.

55. *Paul and the Law*, pp. 264–69, esp. p. 268.

56. "Paul's Conversion," p. 410.

57. Ibid., pp. 410–16.

58. *Paul's Letter to the Romans*, p. 2.

59. Ibid., pp. 39–52.

60. Ibid., pp. 49–50; quotation from p. 50.

61. Ibid., p. 50.

62. *Paul, Judaism and the Gentiles*, p. 178.

63. Ibid., pp. 31–36.

64. Ibid., p. 22.

65. Ibid., pp. 20–21.

66. W. S. Campbell, "Did Paul Advocate Separation from the Synagogue? A Reaction to Francis Watson: *Paul, Judaism and the Gentiles: A Sociological Approach*," *SJT* 42 (1989): 457–67.

67. Thomas R. Schreiner, "'Works of Law' in Paul," *NovT* 33 (1991): 217–44, pp. 237–38.

68. Michael Winger, *By What Law? The Meaning of* Νόμος *in the Letters of Paul*, SBLDS 128 (Atlanta, Ga.: Scholars, 1992).

69. Ibid., pp. 99, 111–12, 123, 153, 167, 199, 201, cited in Thomas R. Schreiner's review of Michael Winger, *By What Law? The Meaning of* Νόμος *in the Letters of Paul*, *JBL* 112 (1993): 724–26.

70. Frank J. Matera, *Galatians*, Sacra Pagina 9 (Collegeville, Minn.: Liturgical Press, 1992).

71. Ibid., p. 11.

72. Ibid., p. 29.

73. Ibid., p. 30.

74. Ibid., pp. 29–30.

75. Ibid., p. 30.

76. Ibid., p. 31.

77. Ibid., pp. 31–32.

78. C. E. B. Cranfield, "Giving a Dog a Bad Name: A Note on H. Räisänen's Paul and the Law, *JSNT* 38 (1990): 77–85.

79. *Israel's Law*, p. 100.

80. Moisés Silva, *Explorations in Exegetical Method: Galatians as a Test Case* (Grand Rapids, Mich.: Baker, 1996), p. 143.

81. Romano Penna, *Paul the Apostle, Volume 2: Wisdom and Folly of the Cross*, Thomas P. Wahl, trans. (Collegeville, Minn.: Liturgical Press, 1996), p. 137; translated from the Italian *L'apostolo Paolo: Studi di esegesi e teologia* (Turin: Edizioni Paolini, 1991).

82. Ibid.

83. Ibid., p. 127, esp. n. 43.

84. Ibid., p. 118.

85. Ibid., p. 127.

86. Ibid., pp. 135–62.

87. R. H. Gundry, "Grace, Works, and Staying Saved in Paul," *Bib* 66 (1985): 1–38.

88. Ibid., p. 36.

89. Ibid., p. 35.

90. Morna D. Hooker, "Paul and 'covenantal nomism,'" *Paul and Paulinism: Essays in Honor of C. K. Barrett*, Morna D. Hooker and S. G. Wilson, eds. (London: SPCK, 1982), pp. 47–56.

91. John J. Collins, *Between Athens and Jerusalem: Jewish Identity in the Hellenistic Diaspora* (New York: Crossroad, 1986).

Chapter 3

1. Jean-François Collange, *L'épître de Saint Paul aux Philippiens*, CNT 10a (Neuchâtel: Delachaux & Niestlé, 1973), p. 115:ET, *The Epistle of Saint Paul to the Philippians*, A. W. Heathcote, trans. (London: Epworth, 1979), p. 130.

2. See, e.g., "Contra Secundinum Manichaeum," *Six traités antiManichéens*, BA:OSA 2/17, R. Jolivet and M. Jourjon, eds. and trans. (Paris: Desclée de Brouwer, 1961), pp. 510–633, p. 630: "non ibi intellecta Dei gratia" (601/xxvi).

3. Augustine, "De gratia Christi et de peccato Originali," *La crise Pélagienne II*, BA:OSA 3/22, J. Plagnieux and F.-J. Thonnard, eds. and trans. (Paris: Desclée de Brouwer, 1975), pp. 9–269, p. 138 (XLII:46).

4. Beker, *Paul the Apostle*, pp. 237–38.

5. Ibid., pp. 242–43.

6. Ibid., p. 341.

7. Ibid., p. 344; for the complete discussion, see pp. 340–47.

8. Ibid., p. 347.

9. George Howard, "Christ the End of the Law," *JBL* 88 (1969): 331–37.

10. George Howard, "Romans 3:21–31 and the Inclusion of the Gentiles," *HTR* 63 (1970): 23–33; see also his *Paul: Crisis in Galatia*, SNTSMS 35 (Cambridge: University Press, 1979), pp. 46–65.

11. Dunn, "The New Perspective on Paul."

12. James D. G. Dunn, "Works of the Law and the Curse of the Law (Galatians 3:10–14)," *NTS* 31 (1985): 523–42.

13. Ibid., p. 523.

14. "Galatians 2.16 and Paul's Break with Judaism," *NTS* 31 (1985): 543–53.

15. "Works of the Law," esp. p. 530; see also "The New Perspective on Paul," and James D. G. Dunn, "The Incident at Antioch," *JSNT* 18 (1983): 2–57.

16. "The New Perspective on Paul," p. 107.

17. Dunn's position in this regard is similar to that of Ambrosiaster, the pseudonym of a fourth-century Latin commentator on Paul, who maintained a distinction between "ritual" or "ceremonial" law and "moral law" in Judaism. See Alexander Souter, *The Earliest Latin Commentaries on the Epistles of St. Paul* (Oxford: Clarendon, 1927), pp. 80–81. See also Robert B. Eno, "Some Patristic Views on the Relationship of Faith & Works in Justification," *RAug* 19 (1984): 3–27, pp. 8–10 and Charles P. Carlson, Jr., *Justification in Earlier Medieval Theology* (The Hague: Martin Nijhoff, 1975), p. 19.

18. Alan F. Segal, *Paul the Convert: The Apostolate and Apostasy of Paul the Pharisee* (New Haven, Conn./London: Yale University, 1990), pp. 124 and 333, n.13.

19. *Romans*, p. 338.

20. *Pistis Christou* has traditionally been translated "faith in Christ," though there has been a recent move, particularly in America, to urge translating the expression as "faith of Christ," commonly said to refer to Christ's obedience. For background on the discussion and a defense of the traditional interpretation, see Veronica Koperski, "The Meaning of *Pistis Christou* in Philippians 3:9," *LS* 18 (1993): 198–216.

21. D. A. Campbell, The Meaning of Πίστις and Νόμος in Paul: A Linguistic and Structural Perspective," *JBL* 111 (1992): 91–103; quotation from pp. 102–3.

22. *From Plight to Solution.*

23. Ibid., p. 24.

24. Schoeps, *Paul*, pp. 184–85; Beker, *Paul the Apostle*, p. 243.

25. *From Plight to Solution*, p. 116.

26. Penna, *Paul the Apostle*, vol. 2, p. 127.

27. *From Plight to Solution*, pp. 28–45.

28. *Between Athens and Jerusalem*, pp. 13–14, 29–30, 48, 77, 141, 167–68, 178, 180, 225.

29. Ibid., p. 14.

30. Ibid., p. 236.

31. H. D. Betz, *Galatians: A Commentary on Paul's Letter to the Churches in Galatia*, Hermeneia (Philadelphia: Fortress, 1979), p. 64.

32. Christopher Rowland, *Christian Origins: An Account of the Setting and Character of the Most Important Messianic Sect of Judaism* (London: SPCK, 1985).

33. Ibid., p. 195.

34. Ibid., pp. 195–97; quotation from p. 197.

35. *Paul the Convert*, e.g., pp. xii, xiv, 6, 20.

36. Leonard Swidler, Lewis John Eron, Gerard Sloyan, and Lester Dean, *Bursting the Bonds? A Jewish-Christian Dialogue on Jesus and Paul*, Faith Meets Faith (Maryknoll, N.Y.: Orbis, 1991), pp. 125–212; see especially the summary, pp. 206–12.

37. Jan Lambrecht, "L'attitude de Paul devant l'heritage spirituel judaïque," *QL* 61 (1980): 195–210.

38. M. Wyschogrod, "Christianity and the Mosaic Law," *Pro Ecclesia* 2 (1993): 451–59.

39. Hendrikus Boers, "'We Who Are by Inheritance Jews; not from the Gentiles, Sinners,'" *JBL* 111 (1992): 273–81, esp. p. 275.

40. Hendrikus Boers, *The Justification of the Gentiles: Paul's Letters to the Galatians and Romans* (Peabody, Mass.: Hendrickson, 1994). The article cited in the previous note includes the major point argued in the book, in much more summary form.

41. E. D. Freed, *The Apostle Paul, Christian Jew: Faithfulness and Law*, rev. ed. (Lanham, Md./New York/London: University Press of America, 1994). The original edition was published in 1986.

42. Daniel Boyarin, *A Radical Jew: Paul and the Politics of Identity*, Contraversions 1 (Berkeley/Los Angeles/London: University of California Press, 1994).

43. N. T. Wright, "Two Radical Jews," *Reviews in Religion and Theology* [London] (3, 1995): 15–23, cited in *New Testament Abstracts* 40 (1996), p. 250, #953r.

44. Terrance Callan, review of *A Radical Jew: Paul and the Politics of Identity* by Daniel Boyarin, *RelSRev* 23 (1997): 300–301.

45. J. D. G. Dunn, review of *A Radical Jew: Paul and the Politics of Identity* by Daniel Boyarin, *relstudNews* 13, no. 1 (Feb. 1998): 1.

46. Daniel Boyarin, "The Jews in Neo-Lutheran Interpretations of Paul," *Dialog* 35 (1996): 193–98.

Chapter 4

1. Brendan Byrne, *"Sons of God"—"Seed of Abraham": A Study of the Idea of the Sonship of God of All Christians in Paul against the Jewish Background* (Rome: Biblical Institute Press, 1979), pp. 227–33.

2. Ibid., pp. 230–31.

3. Ibid., p. 233.

4. Ibid., p. 233.

5. Brendan Byrne, *Romans*, Sacra Pagina 6 (Collegeville, Minn.: Liturgical Press, 1996).

6. For his critique of Räisänen, see *Israel's Law*, p. 217. See pp. 81–86 for his summary of Sanders' views and pp. 217–18 for his expression of agreement with Sanders.

7. See, e.g., ibid., p. 173.

8. Ibid., pp. 114–15.

9. Ibid., pp. 219–22.

10. Ziesler, "Justification," pp. 191–92.

11. *Israel's Law*, p. 222.

12. Brice L. Martin, *Christ and the Law in Paul*, NovTSup 62 (Brill: Leiden/New York/Copenhagen/Cologne, 1989).

13. Eugene Hensell, review of Brice L. Martin, *Christ and the Law in Paul*, *CBQ* 54 (1992): 165–67, p. 165.

14. Frank Thielman, review of Brice L. Martin, *Christ and the Law in Paul*, *JBL* 110 (1991): 349–50; quotation from p. 350.

15. J. Louis Martyn, *Galatians*, AB 33A (New York: Doubleday, 1997).

16. Martin Hengel and Anna Maria Schwemer, *Paul Between Damascus and Antioch* (London: SCM Press, 1997), p. 310.

17. Ibid., p. 313.

18. Ibid., pp. 88–89.

19. G. Bray, "Justification: The Reformers and Recent New Testament Scholarship," *Churchman* 109 (1995): 102–26.

20. K. O. Sandnes, "'Justification by Faith'—An Outdated Doctrine? The 'New Perspective' on Paul—A Presentation and Appraisal," *Theology & Life* (Hong Kong) 17–19 (1996): 127–46.

21. Leon Morris, *Galatians: Paul's Charter of Christian Freedom* (Downers Grove, Ill.: InterVarsity Press, 1996).

22. Colin G. Kruse, *Paul, the Law and Justification* (Peabody, Mass.: Hendrickson, 1996).

23. Gerald F. Hawthorne, *Philippians*, WBC 43 (Waco, Tex.: Word Books, 1983), pp. 140–42. For a different perspective from another evangelical scholar, without argumentation, see Gordon D. Fee, *Paul's Letter to the Philippians*, NICNT (Grand Rapids, Mich.: Eerdmans, 1995), p. 322, n. 35.

24. Silva, *Philippians*, pp. 185–89; see also, for a somewhat different approach, Richard Bevan Hays, *The Faith of Jesus Christ*, SBLDS 56 (Chico, Calif.: Scholars, 1983), pp. 150–51.

25. O'Brien, *Philippians,* pp. 393, 415–17; quotation from p. 417.

26. Ibid., pp. 394–96; quotation from p. 396.

27. Centuries earlier, Augustine had maintained a somewhat similar distinction, asserting that what is to be despised is not really "righteousness coming from Law" or even "Law" (which, for Augustine, is revered as given by God), but rather an improper self-aggrandizing attitude that sees righteousness as the fruit of one's own efforts: the attitude is not one of faith, but of pride, and (here applied to Paul before his Damascus experience) is characterized as not from faith, not according to knowledge, ignorant of God's righteousness. This is the basic argument of most of *Sermon 170* (SAAHEO 5, cols. 818–24) and of a long section of *Sermon 169* SAAHEO 5, cols. 809–14, esp. 813–14 (CLXIX:10). However Augustine also recognized that not all striving for perfect observance of the Law automatically implied an arrogant claim to perfection, citing the examples of Zachary and Elizabeth in the Gospel of Luke in, among other places, *Sermon 169*, SAAHEO 5, cols. 810–11 (CLXIX:6).

28. O'Brien, *Philippians*, p. 397.

29. Ibid., p. 400.

30. Houlden, *Paul's Letters from Prison,* pp. 97–100.

31. James D. G. Dunn, *The Theology of Paul the Apostle* (Grand Rapids, Mich./Cambridge, U.K.: Eerdmans, 1998), pp. 341–42.

32. *Christ and the Law in Paul*, p. 155.

33. Thomas R. Schreiner, "The Abolition and Fulfillment of the Law in Paul," *JSNT* 35 (1989): 47–74, pp. 55–56.

34. Ibid., pp. 55–65.

35. Thomas R. Schreiner, "Works of the Law," *DicPaul*, pp. 975–79, p. 977.

36. For a more recent treatment by Schreiner, see *The Law and Its Fulfillment: A Pauline Theology of Law* (Grand Rapids, Mich.: Baker, 1993).

37. Ibid., p. 241.

38. Dunn, *Theology*, p. 339.

39. Douglas J. Moo, *The Epistle to the Romans*, NICNT (Grand Rapids, Mich./Cambridge, U.K.: Eerdmans, 1996).

40. Ibid., p. 560.

41. Ibid., p. 681.

42. Ibid., p. 298.

43. Jan Lambrecht, review of Douglas J. Moo, *The Epistle to the Romans*, *Bib* 78 (1997): 432–35.

44. Moisés Silva, "Law in the New Testament," *WTJ* 53 (1991): 339–53, esp. 347–53.

45. Silva, *Explorations*, p. 160.

46. Ibid., pp. 148–49.

47. Ibid., p. 160.

48. Ibid., p. 170.

49. Ibid., p. 175.

50. Ibid., pp. 143–50.

51. Ibid., pp. 176–77.

52. Ibid., pp. 187–95.

53. Ibid., pp. 177–80.

54. Karen H. Jobes, "Jerusalem, Our Mother: Metalepsis and Intertextuality in Galatians 4:21–31," *WTJ* 55 (1993): 313–15. Jobes in turn builds on the proposal of Richard B. Hays, *Echoes of Scripture in the Letters of Paul* (New Haven, Conn./London: Yale University Press, 1989), p. 120.

55. Silva, *Explorations*, pp. 180–81.

56. Ibid., pp. 181–84.

57. Here Silva cites in support J. Louis Martyn, "Apocalyptic Antinomies in Paul's Letter to the Galatians," *NTS* 31 (1985): 410–24, pp. 412–14.

58. Here Silva is in agreement with Jeffrey A. D. Weima, "Gal 6:11–18: A Hermeneutical Key to the Galatian Letter," *Calvin Theological Journal* 28 (1993): 90–107, pp. 103–4.

59. Silva, *Explorations*, p. 184.

Chapter 5

1. Jan Lambrecht, "Gesetzesverständnis bei Paulus," *Das Gesetz im Neuen Testament*, QD 108, K. Kertelge, ed. (Freiburg/Basel/Vienna: Herder, 1986), pp. 88–127, p. 109, reprinted in Jan Lambrecht, *Pauline Studies*, BETL 115 (Leuven: Peeters, 1994), pp. 231–270, p. 252.

2. John Buckel, *Free to Love: Paul's Defense of Christian Liberty in Galatians*, LTPM 15 (Louvain/Grand Rapids, Mich.: Peeters/Eerdmans, 1993), p. 129.

3. Ibid., pp. 125–26.

4. Ibid. p. 123.

5. Jan Lambrecht and Richard W. Thompson, *Justification by Faith: The Implications of Romans 3:27–31*, Zacchaeus Studies: New Testament (Wilmington, Del.: Michael Glazier, 1989).

6. Ibid., p. 57. This view has since become more widely held.

7. Ibid., pp. 56–57.

8. Ibid., pp. 57–59; quotation from pp. 58–59.

9. Jan Lambrecht, "Vloek en zegen. Een studie van Galaten 3,10–14," *Collationes* 21 (1991): 133–57, translated into English as "Curse and Blessing: A Study of Galatians 3,10–14," *Pauline Studies*, pp. 271–98, quotation from "Vloek en zegen," p. 151; "Curse and Blessing," p. 289.

10. "The Abolition and Fulfillment of the Law in Paul."

11. *Vloek en zegen*, pp. 151–57, *Curse and Blessing*, pp. 289–96; quotation from final page in each.

12. Byrne, *Romans*, p. 24.

13. Ibid., p. 395.

14. Koperski, "The Meaning of ΔΙΚΑΙΟΣΥΝΗ in Philippians 3:9," pp. 154–68, reprinted with expansions as chapter 4 in Veronica Koperski, *The Knowledge of Christ Jesus My Lord: The High Christology of Philippians 3:7–11*, CBET 16 (Kampen: Kok Pharos, 1996), pp. 191–238.

15. *Knowledge*, chapter 3, pp. 135–90.

16. Ibid., pp. 222–25; "Meaning," pp. 154–57.

17. Ibid., pp. 225–28; "Meaning," pp. 158–61.

18. Ibid., pp. 229–32; "Meaning," pp. 161–63.

19. Ibid., pp. 232–34; "Meaning," pp. 164–66.

20. Ibid., pp. 236–37; "Meaning," p. 168.

21. Ibid., pp. 287–342.

22. Ibid., pp. 293–301. It should be pointed out that the Book of Wisdom is not accepted as canonical in the Protestant tradition. However, I think it most likely that the New Testament writers, Paul included, thought of it as part of their Scripture, as is indicated by, among other things, Paul's reference to Christ crucified as the Wisdom of God in 1 Corinthians 1:24, 30, as well as the use of Wisdom 7 by the author of the Colossians "hymn" in Colossians 1:15–20 and in Hebrews 1:1–3, especially v. 3.

23. Ibid., pp. 301–21. See also Veronica Koperski, "Knowledge of God and Knowledge of Christ in the Corinthian Correspondence," in *The Corinthian Correspondence*, BETL 125, Reimund Bieringer, ed. (Leuven: Peeters, 1996) pp. 183–202, where the "knowledge of God/knowledge of Christ" passages in 1 and 2 Corinthians are explored in greater detail, in comparison with Philippians 3:7–11.

24. Klyne Snodgrass, "Spheres of Influence: A Possible Solution to the Problem of Paul and the Law," *JSNT* 32 (1988): 93–113.

25. Clinton E. Arnold, *Powers of Darkness* (Downers Grove, Ill.: InterVarsity, 1992), p. 132.

26. Joseph A. Fitzmyer, "Pauline Theology," *NJBC*, Raymond E. Brown, Joseph A. Fitzmyer, and Roland E. Murphy, eds. (Englewood Cliffs, N.J.: Prentice-Hall, 1990), pp. 1382–1416, p. 1404, #93.

27. David Wenham, *Paul: Follower of Jesus or Founder of Christianity?* (Grand Rapids, Mich./Cambridge, U.K.: Eerdmans, 1995), p. 226.

28. *Romans*, p. 220.

29. Heinrich Schlier, *Der Römerbrief: Kommentar*, HTKNT 6 (Freiburg im Breisgau: Herder, 1977), p. 234.

30. Ulrich Wilckens, *Der Brief an die Römer*, EKKNT 6, vol. 2 (1980): pp. 89–94.

31. John Paul Heil, *Romans: Paul's Letter of Hope* (Rome: Biblical Institute Press, 1987), p. 48.

32. "Paul and the Law: Why the Law Cannot Save," *NovT* 33 (1991): 35–60.

33. Ibid., p. 53, n. 56.

34. Ibid., pp. 37–38.

35. Ibid., pp. 39–40; quotation from p. 40.

36. Ibid., pp. 46–48.

37. Ibid., pp. 49–51.

38. Cf. 2 Samuel 24:1 with 1 Chronicles 21:1; see also 1 Samuel 16:14; 1 Kings 22:19–23; Psalm 78:49; 1 Corinthians 5:5, 10:10; 2 Corinthians 12:7; Revelation 2:10.

39. "Paul and the Law: Why the Law Cannot Save," pp. 52–53, quotation from p. 53, following Bo Reicke, "The Law and This World According to Paul," *JBL* 70 (1951): 259–76.

40. Jan Lambrecht "Man Before and Without Christ: Rom 7 and Pauline Anthropology," *LS* 5 (1974–75) 18–33, esp. pp. 31–32.

41. Jan Lambrecht, *The Wretched "I" and Its Liberation: Paul in Romans 7 and 8*, LTPM 14 (Louvain/Grand Rapids, Mich.: Peeters/Eerdmans, 1992), pp. 74–78, 84–85.

42. Gerd Theissen, *Psychological Aspects of Pauline Theology*, John P. Galvin, trans. (Edinburgh: T & T Clark, 1987), translated from the German *Psychologische Aspekte paulinischer Theologie*, FRLANT 131 (Göttingen: Vandenhoeck & Ruprecht, 1983), pp. 234–43; quotation from p. 242.

43. Sloan, "Paul and the Law," pp. 53–55.

44. Ibid., pp. 55–56.

45. Ibid., pp. 56–60; quotation from p. 60.

46. Frank Thielman, *Paul and the Law: A Contextual Approach* (Downers Grove, Ill.: InterVarsity, 1994).

47. Thielman, "Law," *DicPaul*, pp. 529–42, pp. 534–42.

48. Although 2 Thessalonians is among the "disputed Paulines," this does not detract substantially from Thielman's presentation, since the only reference unique to 2 Thessalonians is to the "man of lawlessness" in 2:3, 7–8.

49. T. J. Deidun, *New Covenant Morality in Paul*, AnBib 89 (Rome: Biblical Institute, 1981), pp. 10–12, 18–28.

50. Thielman, "Law," p. 535.

51. Ibid., p. 538.

52. Ibid., pp. 538–39.

53. Ibid., pp. 539–40.

54. Ibid., pp. 540–41.

55. Ibid., pp. 540–41; quotation from p. 541.

56. Ibid., pp. 541–42; quotation from p. 542.

57. *Paul*, pp. 54–59, 75–78.

58. It should be noted that the argument depends not simply on the use of the Greek word translated "until" (*heōs* in Mt, *mechri* in Lk), but on the entire context. In Matthew 1:25 (Joseph did not know Mary until [*heōs*] she bore a son), since the context says nothing of Joseph "knowing" Mary later, this cannot be inferred simply from the use of the word translated "until."

59. Ibid., pp. 219–30.

60. Ibid., pp. 255–71.

61. J. D. G. Dunn, "The Justice of God: A Renewed Perspective on Justification by Faith," *JTS* 43 (1992): 1–22; idem, "Paul and Justification by Faith," in R. N. Longenecker, ed., *The Road from Damascus: The Impact of Paul's Conversion on His Life, Thought and Ministry* (Grand Rapids, Mich.: Eerdmans, 1997), pp. 85–101.

62. J. D. G. Dunn, "Echoes of Intra-Jewish Polemic in Paul's Letter to the Galatians," *JBL* 112 (1993): 459–77.

63. J. D. G. Dunn, "Was Paul against the Law? The Law in Galatians and Romans: A Test-Case of Text in Context," in T. Fornberg and D. Hellholm, eds., *Texts and Contexts: Biblical Texts in Their Textual and Situational Contexts*, L. Hartman *Festschrift* (Oslo: Scandinavian University, 1995), pp. 455–75.

64. J. D. G. Dunn, ed., *Paul and the Mosaic Law*, WUNT 89 (Tübingen: Mohr, 1996).

65. Dunn, *Theology*, pp. 128–61.

66. Ibid., pp. 334–89.

67. M. Bachmann, *Sünder oder Übertreter: Studien zur Argumentation in Gal.2.15 ff.*, WUNT 59 (Tübingen: Mohr, 1992), p. 92.

68. Peter Stuhlmacher, *Biblische Theologie des Neuen Testaments 1: Grundlegung von Jesus zu Paulus* (Göttingen: Vandenhoeck & Ruprecht, 1992), p. 264.

69. *Theology*, p. 358, n. 97

70. Ibid., p. 358.

71. Ibid., pp. 159–61.

Chapter 6

1. Peter J. Tomson, *Paul and the Jewish Law: Halakha in the Letters of the Apostle to the Gentiles,* CRINT 3/1 (Minneapolis, Minn.: Fortress, 1990).

2. *Theology*, pp. 722–23.

3. Pp. 441–42.

4. C. J. A. Hickling, "Center and Periphery in Paul's Thought," *Studia Biblica III: Papers on Paul and Other NT Authors*, E. A. Livingstone, ed. (Sheffield: Sheffield Academic Press, 1978), pp. 199–214.

5. *Christ in the Theology of St. Paul*, pp. 4, 509–20, 528–34.

6. Joseph Plevnik, "The Center of Pauline Theology," *CBQ* 51 (1989): 461–78, p. 463.

7. Joseph A. Fitzmyer, *Pauline Theology: A Brief Sketch* (Englewood Cliffs, N.J.: Prentice-Hall, 1967), p. 16. More recently, the same position is set forth in his article "Pauline Theology" in *NJBC*.

8. Ralph P. Martin *Reconciliation: A Study of Paul's Theology* (Atlanta: John Knox, 1981), and, more recently, "Center of Paul's Theology" in *DicPaul*, pp. 92–95, p. 94.

9. Rudolf Schnackenburg, "Christologie des Neuen Testaments," *Mysterium Salutis: Grundriss heilsgeschichtlicher Dogmatik 3/1*, J. Feiner and M. Löhrer, eds. (Einsiedeln/Zurich/Cologne: Benziger, 1970), pp. 227–338, esp. pp. 323–30.

10. Plevnik, "Center," p. 476.

11. Richard B. Gaffin, Jr., *The Centrality of the Resurrection: A Study in Paul's Soteriology* (Grand Rapids, Mich: Baker, 1978).

12. Alister E. McGrath, "Cross, Theology of the," *DicPaul*, pp. 192–97, p. 192.

13. Ernst Käsemann, "The Saving Significance of the Death of Jesus in Paul," *Perspectives on Paul* (London/Philadelphia: SCM/Fortress, 1971), pp. 48, 54.

14. *Theology*, p. 233.

15. Ibid., p. 235.

16. Ibid., p. 237.

17. Ibid., p. 179.

18. Silva, *Explorations*, p. 146.

19. Cited in Richard B. Gaffin, Jr., *The Centrality of the Resurrection*, pp. 19, 21.

20. Albert Schweitzer, *The Mysticism of Paul the Apostle* (New York: Seabury, 1968 [reprint of 1931 ed.]) and *Paul and His Interpreters: A Critical History* (New York: Macmillan, 1912).

21. Herman N. Ridderbos, *Paul: An Outline of His Theology* (Grand Rapids, Mich.: Eerdmans, 1975).

22. *Paul the Apostle.*

23. Ridderbos, *Paul*, p. 39; Beda Rigaux, *Littérature et Théologie Pauliniennes*, RB 5 (Bruges: Desclee Brouwer, 1960).

24. *Theology*, p. 297.

25. R. E. Sturm, "Defining the Word 'Apocalyptic': A Problem in Biblical Criticism," in J. Marcus and Marion L. Soards, eds., *Apocalyptic and the New Testament*, J. L. Martyn *Festschrift*, JSNTSup 24 (Sheffield: Sheffield Academic Press, 1989).

26. R. B. Matlock, *Unveiling the Apocalyptic Paul: Paul's Interpreters and the Rhetoric of Criticism*, JSNTSup 127 (Sheffield: Sheffield Academic Press, 1996).

27. J. Christiaan Beker, *Paul the Apostle: The Triumph of God in Life and Thought*, first paperback ed. (Philadelphia: Fortress, 1984) pp. xiii–xxi; see also p. 58.

28. Nonetheless Silva, in *Explorations*, p. 185, recognizes that one of Beker's main concerns, as expressed in Beker, *Paul the Apostle* (both editions), p. 356, is to preserve the apocalyptic aspects of futurist eschatology.

29. Plevnik, "Center," pp. 473–74.

30. Silva, *Explorations*, p. 149.

31. Martin, "Center," pp. 92–93.

32. Plevnik, "Center," pp. 477–78.

33. *"Righteousness" in the New Testament*, pp. 105–23, 185.

34. John Reumann, *Variety and Unity in New Testament Thought*, Oxford Bible Series (Oxford: University Press, 1991), p. 77.

35. C. A. Davis, *The Structure of Paul's Theology: "The Truth Which Is the Gospel"* (Lewiston, N.Y./Queenston, Ont./Lampeter, U.K.: Mellen Biblical Press, 1995).

36. Martin, "Center," pp. 92–93.

37. Plevnik, "Center," p. 466.

38. Martin, "Center," pp. 93–94.

39. E. E. Lemcio, "The Unifying Kerygma of the New Testament," *JSNT* 36 (1988): 3–17; 38 (1990): 3–11, cited in Martin, "Center," p. 94.

40. *Theology*, p. 231.

41. Koperski, *The Knowledge of Christ Jesus My Lord*, p. 321.

42. *Paul Between Damascus and Antioch*, p. 98.

43. *Paul and Palestinian Judaism*, pp. 441–42.

44. Martin, "Center," p. 94.

45. *Paul Between Damascus and Antioch*, p. 98.

46. *Theology*, p. 179.

47. Ibid., pp. 729–30.

48. Ibid., p. 729.

49. Plevnik, "Center," pp. 477–78.

50. Ibid., pp. 473–74.

51. See, e.g., *Theology*, pp. 266–93.

52. Plevnik, "Center," p. 476.

53. Fitzmyer, *Romans*, p. 111.

54. Ibid., p. 112.

55. Ibid., pp. 110–16.

56. Ibid., pp. 116–24.

57. Reimund Bieringer, "Sünde und Gerechtigkeit," R. Bieringer and J. Lambrecht, *Studies on 2 Corinthians*, BETL 112 (Leuven: Peeters/University Press, 1994), pp. 462–510, p. 510.

58. Koperski, "*Pistis Christou*," pp. 215–16.

Postscript

1. Copyright The Liturgical Conference. All rights reserved. Used with permission.

Bibliography

Earlier Surveys of the Debate on Law in Paul

Barclay, J. M. G. "Paul and the Law: Observations on Some Recent Debates." *Themelios* 12 (1986): 5–15.

Hafemann, S. J. "Paul and His Interpreters." *DicPaul*, pp. 666–79, pp. 671–74.

Moo, Douglas J. "Paul and the Law in the Last Ten Years." *SJT* 40 (1987): 287–307.

Schreiner, Thomas R. "'Works of Law' in Paul." *NovT* 33 (1991): 217–44, pp. 218–38.

Sloan, Robert B. "Paul and the Law: Why the Law Cannot Save." *NovT* 33 (1991): 35–60, esp. pp. 34–45; this is also a major article which attempts to demonstrate consistency in Paul's thinking on the Law, utilizing the notion of "spheres of power" suggested by Klyne Snodgrass.

Soards, Marion L. "The Righteousness of God in the Writings of the Apostle Paul." *BTB* 15 (1985): 104–9; a less technical presentation.

Thielman, Frank. *From Plight to Solution: A Jewish Framework for Understanding Paul's View of the Law in Galatians and Romans.* NovTSup 61. Leiden/New York/Copenhagen/Cologne: E. J. Brill,

1989, pp. 1–27; this is also a major study which argues against E. P. Sanders' notion that, in his references to the Law, Paul was reasoning from solution to plight

————. "Law." *DicPaul*, 529–42, pp. 529–32; a condensed version of the ideas developed in his 1994 monograph, *Paul and the Law: A Contextual Approach.*

Tomson, Peter J. *Paul and the Jewish Law: Halakha in the Letters of the Apostle to the Gentiles*, CRINT 3/1. Assen/Maastricht: Van Gorcum, Minneapolis, Minn.: Fortress, 1990, pp. 5–19; contends that the Law polemic was not a central issue for Paul; scholarly but readable.

Surveys of Paul as a "Christian Jew"

Borgen, Peder. *Philo, John and Paul: New Perspectives on Judaism and Early Christianity.* BJS 131. Atlanta: Scholars, 1987, pp. 233–54.

Riches, John. *Jesus and the Transformation of Judaism.* New York: Seabury, 1982, pp. 112–44.

Thielman, Frank. *From Plight to Solution*, p. 26.

Earlier Discussions of the Center of Paul's Theology

Deidun, T. "Some Recent Attempts at Explaining Paul's Theology." *Way* 26 (1986): 230–42.

Howell, Don N., Jr. "The Center of Pauline Theology." *BSac* 151 (1994): 50–70.

Martin, Ralph P. "Center of Paul's Theology." *DicPaul*, pp. 92–95.

Plevnik, Joseph. "The Center of Pauline Theology." *CBQ* 51 (1989): 461–78.

Selected Writings on Paul and the Law

Badenas, Robert. *Christ the End of the Law: Romans 10:4 in Pauline Perspective.* JSNTSup 10. Sheffield: JSOT, 1985; argues the case that "end" in this context means "goal."

Barclay, J. M. G. "'Do we Undermine the Law?' A Study of Romans 14.1–15.6." In Dunn, ed. *Paul and the Mosaic Law,* pp. 287–308; argues the position that, though Paul fulfills his claim to uphold the law in a limited sense, he regards important aspects of the law as wholly dispensable for Christian believers, and his theology as expressed herein threatens the integrity of those who attempted to live according to the Law.

Boers, Hendrikus. *The Justification of the Gentiles. Paul's Letters to the Galatians and Romans.* Peabody, Mass.: Hendrickson, 1994; uses text-linguistics, structuralism, and semiotics to maintain that the basic concern of Paul in Romans and Galatians is the opposition between justification through works of the Law (limiting salvation to the circumcised) and justification by faith (opening salvation to all); while Boers agrees with Dunn that Paul was consistent in his view of the Law, Boers contends Paul radically misunderstood his Jewish contemporaries.

Brauch, Manfred T. "Perspectives on 'God's righteousness' in recent German discussion." In Sanders, *Paul and Palestinian Judaism,* pp. 523–42; good survey covering the discussion prior to 1977.

Buckel, John. *Free to Love: Paul's Defense of Christian Liberty in Galatians.* LTPM 15. Louvain/Grand Rapids, Mich.: Peeters/Eerdmans, 1993, p. 129; accepts the general position of Sanders and looks for a more theological approach, in opposition to Francis Watson. Written on a somewhat less technical level and thus much more accessible to the nonspecialist reader.

Bultmann, Rudolf. "ΔΙΚΑΙΟΣΥΝΗ ΘΕΟΥ." *JBL* 83 (1964): 12–16; a restatement of the classic Lutheran position on "righteousness of God" originally presented in 1948.

Donfried, K. P., ed. *The Romans Debate: Revised and Expanded Edition.* Peabody, Mass.: Hendrickson, 1991. Some of the essays within this volume are relevant to the topic of the Law. In addition, recent major commentaries on Romans and Galatians will provide an abundance of material, as well as further bibliography.

Dunn, James D. G. "The New Perspective on Paul." *BJRL* 65 (1983): 94–122; follows the line of Sanders, whom Dunn hails as having been a major catalyst of the "new perspective"; however, Sanders is criticized for perceiving an unwarranted degree of inconsistency in Paul's view of the Law. Dunn argues that the "works of the Law" that are problematic for Paul refer to identity markers such as circumcision and observance of food laws.

————. "Works of the Law and the Curse of the Law (Galatians 3:10–14)." *NTS* 31 (1985): 523–42; criticizes Räisänen for viewing Paul as inconsistent and argues that one must take into account the complexity of the situations Paul faced; in Galatians, Dunn maintains, Paul is arguing against a wrong *attitude* toward the Law.

————ed. *Paul and the Mosaic Law.* WUNT 89. Tübingen: Mohr, 1996; the proceedings of the Third Durham-Tübingen Research Symposium on Earliest Christianity and Judaism, held in Durham, September, 1994, includes opening and closing ("In Search of Common Ground") articles by Dunn, as well as articles by Hermann Lichtenberger, Martin Hengel, Jan Lambrecht, Bruce Longenecker, Graham Stanton, Karl Kertelge, N. T. Wright, Richard B. Hays, Otfried Hofius, Hans Hübner, Stephen Westerholm, Heikki Räisänen, Peter J. Tomson, Stephen C. Barton, and John M. G. Barclay, several conceived as responses to other articles within the volume. Somewhat more challenging reading, but an opportunity to get the flavor of scholars engaged in their craft.

————. *The Theology of Paul the Apostle.* Grand Rapids, Mich./Cambridge, U.K: Eerdmans, 1998, pp. 128–61 and 334–89; sections on the Law and justification by faith summarize Dunn's views through the years, with responses to criticism of his positions by other scholars.

Fitzmyer, Joseph A. "Pauline Theology." *NJBC*, Raymond E. Brown, Joseph A. Fitzmyer, and Roland E. Murphy, eds. (Englewood Cliffs, N.J.: Prentice-Hall, 1990), pp. 1382–1416; p. 1404, #93 deals with the Law in Paul in summary fashion; see also Fitzmyer's commentary on Romans in *NJBC* and *Romans: A New Translation with Introduction and Commentary.* AB 33. Doubleday: New York/London/Toronto/Sydney/Auckland: 1993.

Hooker, Morna D. "Paul and 'covenantal nomism.'" In *Paul and Paulinism: Essays in Honor of C. K. Barrett*, Morna D. Hooker and S. G. Wilson, eds. London: SPCK, 1982, pp. 47–56 (reprinted in Hooker, *From Adam to Christ,* Cambridge, U.K./New York: Cambridge University, 1990, pp. 155–64); a balanced critique of Sanders' *Paul and Palestinian Judaism.*

Howard, George. "Christ the End of the Law," *JBL* 88 (1969): 331–37 and "Romans 3:21–31 and the Inclusion of the Gentiles," *HTR* 63 (1970): 23–33; an earlier version of a position later made influential by J. D. G. Dunn: the problem of the Law for Paul is that it separates Jews from Gentiles.

Hübner, Hans. *Law in Paul's Thought*, James Greig, trans. Edinburgh: T. & T. Clark, 1984; based on *das Gesetz bei Paulus*. Göttingen: Vandenhoeck & Ruprecht, 1978, which distinguishes between Paul's view of the Law in Galatians and Romans.

Käsemann, Ernst. "The Righteousness of God in Paul," *New Testament Questions of Today.* New Testament Library. London: SCM, 1969, pp. 168–82; the English translation is based on a later German version appearing in *Exegetische Versuche und Besinnungen*. Göttingen: Vandenhoeck & Ruprecht, ²1965, pp. 181–93, and includes in the notes a reaction to Bultmann's 1964 article in *JBL*.

Klein, Günter. "Righteousness in the New Testament." *IDBSup*, pp. 750–52; a history of discussion on righteousness up to 1976.

Koperski, Veronica. "The Meaning of ΔΙΚΑΙΟΣΥΝΗ in Philippians 3:9." *The Ministry of the Word: Essays in Honor of Prof. Dr. Raymond F. Collins*, Joseph A. Selling, ed., *LS* 20 (1995): 147–69, pp. 154–68; a close discussion of a passage frequently referred to in the discussion of righteousness and the Law in Paul, but not previously studied in detail.

Lambrecht, Jan, and Richard W. Thompson. *Justification by Faith: The Implications of Romans 3:27–31.* Zacchaeus Studies: New Testament. Wilmington, Del.: Michael Glazier, 1989; these scholars maintain, in opposition to Dunn, that Paul was concerned with upholding the entire law, ceremonial aspects included, and that, in reinterpreting such ceremonial aspects, he was actually upholding the Law.

Lambrecht, Jan. "Curse and Blessing: A Study of Galatians 3:10–14." *Pauline Studies*, BETL 115. Leuven: Peeters, 1994, pp. 271–98; a translation of an article that appeared in Flemish in *Collationes* in 1991; combines elements from various, sometimes competing, approaches to the issue of Paul and the Law.

Matera, Frank J. *Galatians.* Sacra Pagina 9. Collegeville, Minn.: Liturgical Press, 1992; a concerted effort to demonstrate the theological value and contemporary significance of the Letter to the Galatians within the discussion of the Law.

Olley, John W. *"Righteousness" in the Septuagint of Isaiah: A Contextual Study.* SBLSCS 8. Missoula, Mont.: Scholars, 1979; provides some Old Testament background that is helpful in attempting to contextualize the New Testament discussion.

Räisänen, Heikki. *Paul and the Law.* WUNT 29. Tübingen: J. C. B. Mohr, 1983; a major study in the line of Sanders, which, however, has been criticized for portraying Paul as hopelessly inconsistent.

———. "Paul's Conversion and the Development of His View of the Law." *NTS* 33 (1987): 404–19; somewhat attempts to defend Paul from being inconsistent by arguing that his view on the Law changed gradually as a result of polemic.

Reumann, John. *"Righteousness" in the New Testament: "Justification" in the United States Lutheran–Roman Catholic Dialogue,* with responses by Joseph A. Fitzmyer and Jerome D. Quinn. Philadelphia, Pa./New York: Fortress/Paulist, 1982; an attempt to appreciate opposite perspectives.

Ropes, James Hardy. "'Righteousness' and 'The Righteousness of God' in the Old Testament and in St. Paul." *JBL* 22 (1903): 211–27; Ropes evidences familiarity with the contemporaneous German discussion and provides bibliography and/or bibliographical sources dealing with the issue.

Sanders, E. P. *Paul and Palestinian Judaism: A Comparison of Patterns of Religion*. London/Philadelphia, Pa.: SCM/Fortress, 1977; though not the first to argue against the Lutheran view of ancient Judaism as a religion of works, this book appeared at a time when the scholarly world was more open to an alternative interpretation and became influential in promoting a "new perspective" on Paul.

———. *Paul, the Law and the Jewish People*. Philadelphia, Pa./London: Fortress/SCM, 1983/1985; further development of the ideas in *Paul and Palestinian Judaism*.

Sandnes, K. O. "'Justification by Faith'—An Outdated Doctrine? The 'New Perspective' on Paul—A Presentation and Appraisal." *Theology & Life* (Hong Kong) 17–19 (1996): 127–46; a recent restatement of the Lutheran stress on justification by faith as the core of Christian theology, though with some openness to the idea that this emphasis may sometimes be too strongly focused on salvation of the individual.

Silva, Moisés. *Explorations in Exegetical Method: Galatians as a Test Case*. Grand Rapids, Mich.: Baker 1996; the author's views on Law in Galatians emerge in a methodological study which recognizes that each interpreter comes to the text with a perspective which affects exegesis.

Snodgrass, Klyne. "Spheres of Influence: A Possible Solution to the Problem of Paul and the Law." *JSNT* 32 (1988): 93–113; reprinted in *The Pauline Writings*, Stanley E. Porter and Craig A. Evans, eds., The Biblical Seminar 34, Sheffield: Sheffield Academic

Press, 1995; an influential article that articulates in more detail a notion independently recognized by a number of scholars; Snodgrass suggests that, in the discussion of Paul's apparently inconsistent statements about the Law, one should recognize that, for Paul, the determinant for the Law is the sphere in which it is located. While its rightful use is in the sphere of Christ, it can be "taken over" and used by sin.

Soards, Marion L. "Käsemann's 'Righteousness' Reexamined." CBQ 47 (1987): 264–67; disagrees with Käsemann's interpretation based on the use of the term "righteousness" in pre-Christian texts.

Thielman, Frank. *Paul and the Law: A Contextual Approach*. Downers Grove, Ill.: InterVarsity, 1994; examines Paul's view of the Law in the contexts of Judaism, the circumstances of the letters, and the language and argumentation of each letter, concluding that Paul's position on the Law was a complex evolution of his conviction that the Mosaic Law is the authoritative word of God, a word that has nonetheless been interpreted by the Spirit in unforeseen ways.

Watson, Francis. *Paul, Judaism and the Gentiles: A Sociological Approach*. SNTSMS 56. Cambridge/London/New York/Melbourne: Cambridge University, 1986; while the sociological approach presents an interesting perspective, Watson's lack of attention to theological background in Paul has been criticized.

Westerholm, Stephen. *Israel's Law and the Church's Faith: Paul and His Recent Interpreters*. Grand Rapids, Mich.: Eerdmans, 1988; while open to some of the ideas of Sanders, this work basically defends the Lutheran position.

Winger, Michael. *By What Law? The Meaning of* Νόμος *in the Letters of Paul*. SBLDS 128. Atlanta, Ga.: Scholars, 1992; attempts to determine the meaning of *nomos* using lexical semantics; however, Winger has been criticized for overemphasis on sociological aspects to the neglect of the theological dimension.

Wright, N. T. *The Climax of the Covenant: Christ and the Law in Pauline Theology.* Minneapolis, Minn.: Fortress, 1992; argues for a positive sense of Law as leading to Christ.

Ziesler, J. A. *The Meaning of Righteousness in Paul: A Linguistic and Theological Enquiry.* Cambridge, U.K.: University Press, 1972; a major linguistic study; at this point Ziesler was still leaning toward the traditional Lutheran interpretation.

———. *Paul's Letter to the Romans*, TPI New Testament Commentaries, London/Philadelphia, Pa.: SCM/Trinity Press International, 1989, and "Justification by Faith," *Theology* 94 (1991): 188–94; two writings that reflect a change in Ziesler's perspective as a result of dialog with E. P. Sanders.

Author Index

Ambrosiaster, 118
Andressen, Carl, 108
Arnold, Clinton E., 75, 124
Augustine, vii, x, 20, 37, 112,
 115, 117, 121

Bachmann, M., 91, 126
Badenas, Robert, 24–25, 114, 132
Barclay, J. M. G., 130, 132–33
Barrett, C. K., 110, 117, 134
Barth, Karl, 7, 51, 108
Barton, Stephen C., 133
Bassler, Jouette, 12, 110
Baur, F. C., 3, 93, 107
Beare, Francis Wright, 10 –11,
 14 –15, 22, 109, 111
Bechtler, Steven Richard, 24, 26,
 114
Becker, Jürgen, 25, 114
Beker, J. Christiaan, 3, 13, 37–39,
 41, 95–97, 100–101, 107,
 110, 117–18, 128
Betz, H. D., 43–44, 118
Bieringer, Reimund, 102, 124,
 129

Boers, Hendrikus, 43, 45, 119,
 132
Borgen, Peder, 131
Boyarin, Daniel, 43, 45–46, 119
Brauch, Manfred T., 12, 110, 132
Braun, Herbert, 25, 114
Bray, G., 52, 120
Bromiley, Geoffrey, xi
Brown, Raymond E., 124, 134
Bruce, F. F., 113–14
Buckel, John, 66–67, 123, 132
Bultmann, Rudolf, 4–5, 7–9,
 10–13, 18–19, 22, 48, 50,
 52–54, 56, 64–65, 73,
 107–9, 113, 132, 134
Byrne, Brendan, 13, 48–49,
 70–71, 75, 110, 120, 123

Callan, Terrance, 45, 119
Calvin, John, 51
Campbell, D. A., 41, 118
Campbell, W. S., 31, 116
Carlson, Charles P., Jr., 118
Cerfaux, Lucien, 10, 12, 94, 109
Chrysostom, John, 9, 108

Scripture Index